The Curiosity Club™

Kids' Nature Activity Book

Written and Illustrated by
Allene Roberts

John Wiley & Sons, Inc.

New York · Chichester · Brisbane · Toronto · Singapore

The Curiosity Club™ is a trademark of Allene Roberts and Teresa Hartnett.

Copyright © 1992 by Allene Roberts.

Published by John Wiley & Sons, Inc.

ISBN 0-471-55589-4

Printed in the United States of America

10 9 8 7 6 5 4 3

For
John Owen
Roberts

Preface

This book is designed to quicken childrens' curiosity and to spark their imaginations. It has plenty of pictures to help the printed words come alive. Younger children might enjoy this book as they would a story book, looking at the pictures while an adult reads the text. Older children may prefer to go it alone.

The projects are simple, using materials easily found around the house. A child will be able to do many of the projects alone, and when an adult's help is needed, it's clearly stated. But why not use this book as a family resource? For example, you can turn collecting wild plant seeds into a family project, setting aside space for wild plants in your garden. Or, if you live in a place where that's not possible, you can make family projects out of watching bird behavior when you see sparrows sparring on the sidewalk or finding clues in cloud formations of weather to come. Make a wind sock to hang outside a window and make a point of looking at it together before your family's day begins. Is there a wind? Where is it blowing from? Where did the wind come from yesterday?

Many projects will provide children with good reasons for going outside. There are also pencil-and-paper activities, role-playing games, and observation projects for time indoors.

As adults we are always trying to find ways to teach our children important values. We carefully rinse out bottles for recycling and teach our children to do the same. And we know that children know the difference between a task done as a dull chore and a task done gladly, out of a growing love for the natural world. So as we rinse, we think about the landfill space we don't use up when we recycle.

But we really don't have to say much to our children about environmental issues, especially when they are very young. Why tell them in a negative way about municipal landfills, when a positive delight in making a dog out of burdocks with your child expresses your love for the earth much more eloquently?

We want our children to love the natural world as much as or maybe even more than we do. Love for any thing or any person doesn't often happen all at once, does it? It happens a little bit here, a little bit there.

Love for the natural world happens when you watch sow bugs turn leaves into soil, and when you feel a tree's bark with your fingers underneath the rubbing you just made. It happens when the sky suddenly turns into an ocean of air in your imagination, and trees become seaweed and birds become fish swimming through the air currents. It happens when you blow on a strip of paper and suddenly understand how a bird can lift off the ground and fly through the air with nothing more than a web of skin and feathers.

As I write this, a crow is playing with the wind outside my window. He swoops down low, then loops back up, flapping steadily against the stiff wind. Then he soars up high over the telephone pole and swoops down again. I can almost hear him laughing. He plays with the wind, our children run outside to play, and we play outside too, whenever we can. May all of us share the same delight in the natural world!

Acknowledgments

Many individuals and institutions have aided in making this book. The good qualities of this book have many sources; any flaws are my own. I wish to thank especially:

The Monroe County Parks Department;

The Monroe County Library System

The Rochester Museum and Science Center;

Michelle French and Sybil Prince for their cheerful and reliable help, and Sybil Prince also for the beautiful tree drawing on page 11;

Members of the Curiosity Club™ for their help in choosing activities;

My parents, for giving me a love of the natural world;

My husband, Russell, for his practical advice and loving companionship;

Edith Sisson, for her careful and detailed comments;

Mary Daniello, Laura Cleveland, and all who together have done such excellent work on the challenging task of turning a manuscript and artwork into a finished book; and

Kate C. Bradford, my editor, for her excellent advice and encouragement.

I am also deeply grateful to Elise Bninski and Teresa Hartnett for the gift of their loving encouragement and practical help that began on a long-ago October evening.

Allene Roberts

Mendon, New York
May 1992

Contents

INTRODUCTION   1

CHAPTER 1

Trees
3

CHAPTER 2

*Green
Plants
25*

CHAPTER 3

*Soil
47*

CHAPTER 4

*Animals
65*

CHAPTER 5

*Birds
95*

CHAPTER 6

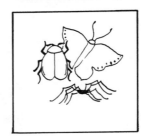

*Insects
and
Spiders
121*

CHAPTER 7

*Weather
149*

**RESOURCES: MORE THINGS
TO DO**   180

LIST OF ACTIVITIES   182

INDEX   183

INTRODUCTION

- *Do you think the air smells good after a cool rain?*
- *Do you like to look at the sky?*
- *Do you talk back to squirrels?*

This book is for you if you answered "yes" to any of these questions. But if you answered any or all of them with a "no," don't feel left out. Maybe you live in a place that doesn't get much rain. Maybe you live in a city and have to stretch a lot to see anything other than tall buildings. Maybe a squirrel has never scolded you for walking under his tree.

You may not realize how you feel about the natural world because you don't have many chances to experience what happens out-of-doors. But even in the biggest city, even in your back yard if you have one, even on the driest desert, clouds come and go, plants grow, and animals hunt for food and raise their little ones.

It is possible to walk through any of these places, and even through the wildest of places, without seeing much of anything. Many people do just that. But I've watched a raccoon amble up to the edge of a birthday party in a park to find food. Nobody saw the raccoon except me. Later I found an animal run in the weeds a few feet away. What is an animal run, and what can it tell you about animals? Find out in the chapter on animals!

You can learn to see things many people miss. Learning about the natural world is like getting a strange new pair of glasses. As you learn more, you will see more. And more. And more. And more. It never stops!

How can you learn about the natural world? There are two ways, and you need them both. The first is by learning what people can teach you—through magazines, television, school, people you meet, and through books.

The second way is by *really* being outdoors. Lots of people walk or jog outdoors, but they are really thinking about other things. The next time you are outdoors, even if it's only for a minute, ask yourself, "What can I see and hear, smell and touch that I usually don't?" You may be surprised.

Sometimes people need a reason to be outside. This book has lots of activity suggestions that will give you good reasons to be outside. You can go outside to find leaves to use as stencils, to find a chicory plant that will tell you what kind of weather might be coming, or to look for animal tracks. You can go outdoors to find some sow bugs (so you can watch them make soil at your leisure), catch a moth at night, or watch a dandelion go from flower to seedhead. You can go outside to put a fresh supply of hair from your family's hairbrushes in the crook of a tree to help birds make their nests.

There are also lots of puzzles, word games, and imagination games you can do when you can't go outside.

The activities mostly call for things you can find around the house, in a park, or in your back yard. You can do many of them on your own, without an adult's help. But if you feel like it, see if you can find an adult to share a project with you anyway. Why not make a wind sock together? Or have a contest to see who can see the most animals from a place outside that you pick together? Adults need some fun in their lives, too.

I think that the natural world talks to us. It's not a language like Spanish, English, or Chinese. It's a language with very different words.

You can touch a crinkly new leaf in the spring, and there's a word. You don't have to put it into people language to understand it, do you? You can watch a cloud flowing across the sky, changing shape, and there's another word. Find a patch of slippery clay at a tree's roots, and there's another "natural" word.

- *What natural words do you know already?*
- *What new natural words will you learn?*

CHAPTER 1

Trees

Why Do We Need Trees?

When you were a tiny baby, just born, you began to do something that you have never stopped doing. All the time between then and now you have been doing it. What are you doing right now that's so important?

BREATHING!

Trees and other green plants that lived millions of years ago and trees that live today have given you the gift that you need to breathe. What is that gift?

BREATHABLE AIR!

A long, long time ago the air on the surface of the earth was very different from the way it is today. Trees and other plants could use that air, but animals and people could not. So there were no animals or people back then. But, very slowly, as trees grew, used the air, and did their work, they put something very important into the air that made it possible for animals and people to live and breathe today.

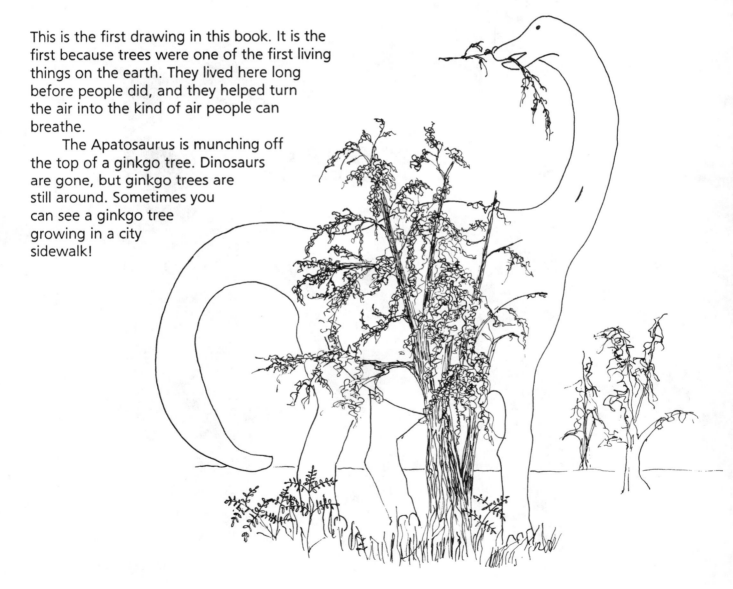

This is the first drawing in this book. It is the first because trees were one of the first living things on the earth. They lived here long before people did, and they helped turn the air into the kind of air people can breathe.

The Apatosaurus is munching off the top of a ginkgo tree. Dinosaurs are gone, but ginkgo trees are still around. Sometimes you can see a ginkgo tree growing in a city sidewalk!

What Is Air?

You can't see the air or feel it with your fingers. Air is a mixture of things we cannot see or touch. These things are called **gases**. You may have heard of nitrogen or carbon dioxide. They are gases that are part of the air. They are "inside" the air.

Have you ever mixed blue and yellow paint together to get green? Even though your mixture is green, you know that the yellow paint and the blue paint are "inside" the green paint. Different kinds of gases are "inside" the air we breathe in the same way.

You have probably heard of **oxygen**. That is the gas "inside" the air that we and all living animals need to stay alive. Oxygen is the special gift that trees and other plants give to us.

How Are Trees Like People?

Trees and other plants are like people in a lot of ways. As you know, they need water and air to live just like you do. They love the sun, too. They grow straight up toward the sun just like you are doing now!

Trees also "breathe" and "eat," but not in exactly the same way that you do.

How Do Trees "Breathe"?

You take air inside you when you take a breath through your mouth or your nose. But when you look at a tree, no matter how carefully, you won't see a mouth or a nose! So how does the air the trees need get into their insides?

You can see where a tree takes in air by looking at any leaf carefully. Compare the way the top of the leaf looks (the side the sun shines on) with the underside (bottom). How are the two sides different?

You may notice that the top side of the leaf is shinier than the underside. That's because the top side of the leaf is covered with a kind of wax that lets the sunshine through to the inside part of the leaf, but keeps out the rain.

Keeping the rain from soaking the leaf is important. You can't breathe in water and neither can a tree. On the underside of the leaf are lots of tiny "windows" that you usually can't see without a microscope. This is where the air gets in. If the windows were clogged with rainwater they couldn't let the air into the inside of the plant.

A Different Way to Color!

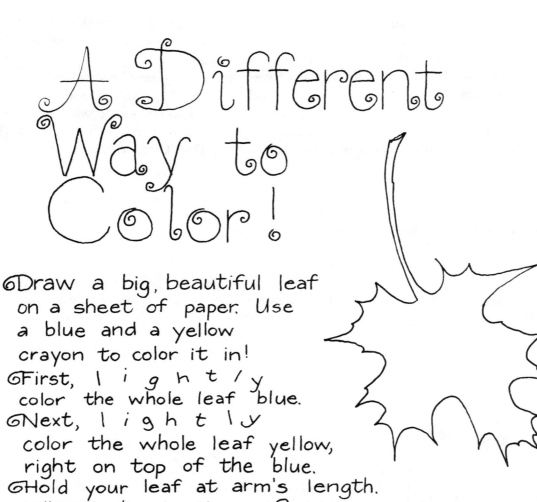

6 Draw a big, beautiful leaf on a sheet of paper. Use a blue and a yellow crayon to color it in!

6 First, l i g h t l y color the whole leaf blue.

6 Next, l i g h t l y color the whole leaf yellow, right on top of the blue.

6 Hold your leaf at arm's length. What color is it now?

6 Here is some "pretend math" to think about:

blue + yellow = green

* * * * * * * * * * * * * * * * * *

carbon dioxide + oxygen + lots of

other gases = A I R !!!

And here is something especially neat: As you know, the air is a mixture of gases, including carbon dioxide and oxygen. Trees and other plants "breathe" *in* carbon dioxide and "breathe" *out* oxygen. But animals and people breathe *in* oxygen and breathe *out* carbon dioxide.

The grass in your yard, the trees on your street, and the dandelions in the cracks of the sidewalk give animals and people oxygen to breathe. Corn growing on the prairie, cacti in the desert, rain forests growing where it is really hot, even algae in the ocean "breathe" out oxygen.

Trees and other plants, animals, and people all help each other.

How Do Trees "Eat"?

Trees and other plants need food, but they get it in a very different way than we do. Did you ever see a tree eat a peanut-butter-and-jelly sandwich?

Maybe you have eaten lots of peanut-butter-and-jelly sandwiches in your day. Now think: Where does peanut butter come from? What about jelly? And bread is made from flour. Where does the flour come from?

You guessed it. They all come from plants! Peanut plants, grapevines, apple trees, or raspberry bushes! Wheat growing in big fields! Even if you eat meat, the animals the meat came from needed plants to eat.

This is where we get our food. But did you know that plants make their own food? They are the only living things that do. How do they do it?

Why Are Trees Green?

Plants, including trees, make their food out of three things: air, water, and, amazingly, sunlight. The food they make for themselves is a kind of sugar. It's not white and grainy, like the sugar we use at the table. It's their own special kind of sugar, which you can sometimes see as a tree's sap.

You may know how maple syrup is made from the sugar maple tree's sap. All trees have sap, an important liquid that flows between a tree's leaves and roots. The sap carries the tree's sugar. Different kinds of trees make exactly the kind of sugar and sap they need to live and grow.

Trees and other plants make their sugar out of carbon, hydrogen, and oxygen. They pull carbon and oxygen from the air and hydrogen and oxygen from the water they drink up through their roots.

But the tree needs energy to pull apart the air and water. That's where the sunlight comes in!

Plants have something called **chlorophyll** in their leaves. Chlorophyll is very special. It is what traps the sunlight in a plant's leaves and turns the sunlight's energy into the kind of energy that can pull apart the air and water and put the pieces back together again to make sugar, the plant's food.

Chlorophyll is also what makes a plant look green. Even plants that don't look green, like red maples or coleus, have chlorophyll. The chlorophyll's green color is just overpowered by the plant's other colors.

Plants are the only living things that can make their own food, and we still don't completely understand how they can do it. So plants give us the air and the food that we need to live. And they give us a mystery, too! Maybe you can help to discover their secrets.

How do plants make their own food?

Use your own paper to write the answers to each question.

1. What's inside the "empty" glass?

2. What's "inside" the answer to No. 1? (Two answers.)

3. This glass stood outside in a rainstorm. What's inside this glass?

4. What's "inside" the answer to No. 3? (Two answers.)

5.

What turns hydrogen, oxygen, and carbon into sugar? (Hint: it makes plants look green.)

6. So... (Three answers)

 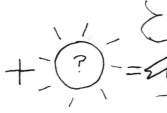 

Tall Green Friends

It often happens that the more we learn about people, the more we like them. You have just learned a lot about trees. How would you like to make a tree your very own friend?

Have you ever noticed a special tree in your yard or on your way to school or in your neighborhood? To adopt a tall green friend, you need a tree you can visit up close any time you want.

It's fun to begin a journal about your tree. The following pages will give you lots of ideas about what you can put in your journal. Sometimes there are questions about your friend that you can answer in your journal, and sometimes there are suggestions for ways you can take "snapshots" of your tree. Once you really get to know your tall green friend, you will begin to get lots of ideas on your own!

Draw Your Friend

Begin your journal with a drawing of your tall green friend. Artists say they learn a lot about the people they draw even if they don't know them before they begin the drawing. You can learn a lot about your friend just by drawing your tree carefully.

A good rule to keep in mind when you "draw from life" is to look at what you are drawing two-thirds of the time and spend only one-third looking at your paper. You don't need to look at a watch to do this. Just keep your eyes on the tree most of the time, so you notice how the branches grow from the trunk, where the leaves grow from the branches, and how the bark looks. Then draw a quick sketch of what you have seen.

You have learned a lot about your friend, haven't you? Date your drawing. When you do other drawings you can compare how your tree looks in different seasons.

Talking Trees

You talk a lot with your friends. Can you talk with a tree? A tree won't speak your language, but maybe you can learn to listen to a tree's way to talking. You will need your ears to listen, of course. But your eyes, nose, and fingers can "listen" to a tree's talking, too. The drawing on page 12 may help you to learn about a tree's way of talking.

Using Your Ears to Listen

Sometimes when you go to visit your tall green friend, you can decide to use only your ears to listen to your friend talk. What do you hear your friend saying? Write down what you hear in your journal.

Here are some questions to help you tune your ears:

■ If there is a breeze, do you hear the branches rubbing together, the leaves, or both?
■ Can you hear insects?

Here is a tree that grows in Sybil's back yard. She made this drawing in the winter. What kind of a tree do you think it is?

What is a tree saying to you?

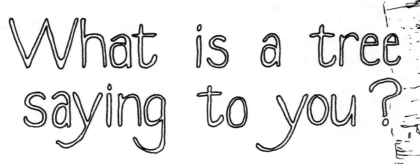

Sometimes when you talk with your friends, you say things fast and you listen fast. And sometimes longer conversations are good.

But a tree's language isn't as quick as ours. To talk and listen in tree language, you need a lot of time, and you need your eyes and nose and fingers to listen, too.

What does a tree say to you when its leaves are talking in the wind?

Can you smell a tree's words when it blooms in the spring? Can you smell your tree's words on a hot summer day? Maybe the tree's words are a little damp, a little cool.

A tree's bark says lots of words. Close your eyes and "listen" with your fingers.

You can't really say in human words what tree words say, but you know what a tree says, just the same.

- Can you hear birds in your tree?
- Can you hear animals in your tree?

You can write down what you hear in words, or in sounds. (Does a squirrel say "CHIRRRR" when it scolds you?) Write down whatever will help you to remember the sounds when you read your journal a month from now. Pictures can help you remember, too.

Looking at Parts of Trees

Get to know the different parts of your friend. People have toes, legs, and a middle (which we sometimes call our "trunk," just like a tree!). We have arms, hands, fingers, and a head. All these parts together make a whole person.

Trees have different parts, too. All together these parts make a whole tree. Can you name the parts of your tall green friend?

Roots

There is no good way to look at your friend's roots. That's because most of the roots are under the soil. The only way we usually see roots at all is by digging, but don't try this because you might harm your tree.

Roots are very important in two ways. The first is, roots hold a tree up, just like your feet hold you up! What would happen to your friend if your tree's roots suddenly disappeared?

The second reason roots are important to a tree is because through the roots, the tree gets most of the water it needs. Many of the minerals it needs to live are dissolved in the water it pulls through its roots.

You can't put a tree root in your journal, but you can take an imaginary journey under the soil. You know how it feels to wiggle your bare toes in sand at the beach, or in grass, or in dirt. Imagine your toes are turning into roots and are growing down, down, down into the earth. Here are some questions to get you started in your journal entry about your tree's roots.

- How do your roots feel when they are moist?
- What do your roots do when they find a stone?
- Are there any animals down there among your roots?

Trunk and Bark

How big is your friend's trunk? Is it big enough to put your hands around? Is it big enough to put your arms around? Is it bigger than THAT?

In some ways, your friend's bark is like your skin. It protects a tree's insides just like your skin protects your insides.

Little nicks and scratches in a tree's bark don't hurt the tree. Sometimes carefully taking off a branch or two actually helps a tree. That's called **pruning**. But if you took the bark off all around the tree, the tree would die. So bark is very important.

What is your friend's bark like? Feel it with your fingers. Is it bumpy or smooth? Is it a thin layer on the tree, or is it thick, like a dog with a shaggy coat? Is it a dark color or a light color? The kind of bark a tree has can tell you a lot about the kind of tree it is.

You have probably noticed that some bark is very bumpy. Even trees with the smoothest bark are more wrinkly than your own skin. Why?

Have you ever taken a mitten or a sock you wore when you were a lot smaller, or maybe a younger brother or sister's sock, and put it on your big hand or foot? What happens?

It stretches very tight! Sometimes you can't even get your hand or foot all the way inside. It stretches so tight that you can even see the stitches in the mitten or sock that you didn't notice before.

The same thing happens to bark as a tree gets older and bigger. It s-t-r-e-t-c-h-e-s. And each kind of tree's bark stretches in its own way and makes its own pattern of stretched bark.

Close your eyes when you feel your tree's bark. Are your fingertips sensitive enough to feel each "hill and valley" on the surface of your tree's trunk? If someone led you blindfolded to several different trees, could you recognize your tree just by touching it?

Take a "snapshot" of your tree's bark with a bark rubbing. The drawing on this page shows you how.

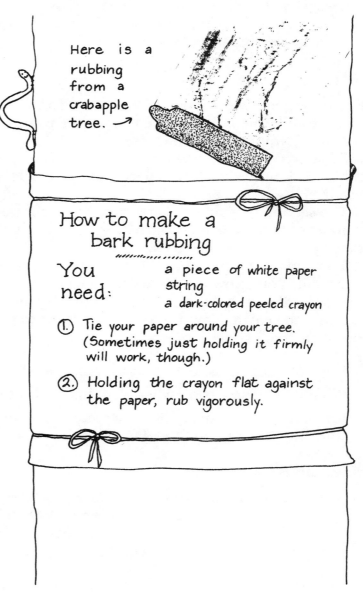

Here is a rubbing from a crabapple tree. →

How to make a bark rubbing

You need: a piece of white paper
string
a dark-colored peeled crayon

1. Tie your paper around your tree. (Sometimes just holding it firmly will work, though.)

2. Holding the crayon flat against the paper, rub vigorously.

Branches

Stand up close to your friend's trunk. As close as you can. Are you about to hug your tree? Now look UP!

Here are some questions to help you learn about your friend's branches.

■ Does your friend have one big trunk reaching up to the sky? Or does your friend have lots of smaller branches that aren't really big enough to be called trunks? Can you count them?

■ When you stand a long way away from your tree, could you fit your tree inside an imaginary circle? If it doesn't fit, try an imaginary square, a triangle, or a rectangle.

■ Do you see any other trees around your tree that could fit into that same imaginary shape? Are they the same kind of tree as your tall green friend?

These questions can help you see how your tree shares a pattern with other trees of the same kind. By answering these questions you may be able to recognize other trees that are just like your friend just by looking at their branching patterns. Every kind of tree has its own way of growing its branches out so its leaves can get the most sun.

What time of year would be the best for seeing branching patterns in broadleaf trees, summer or winter?

Leaves

Before you use these questions to help you to get to know your friend's leaves a little better, you need to answer one BIG question first: Is your tree a broadleaf or a conifer? (Or maybe a palm or a cactus?) Turn to pages 18 and 19 if you need help to answer.

Here are some questions to help you to get to know your friend's leaves better:

■ What color are your friend's leaves? (For example, are they green, or green-yellow, or green-blue?)

■ How would you describe the shape of your friend's leaves? Can you draw the exact shape?

■ Are the leaves smooth on their edges, or do the edges look like the edge of a saw, with "teeth"?

- Are the leaves simple or compound? (See the drawings for examples of each kind of leaf.)

- What kind of pattern does your tree use when it holds its leaves out toward the sun? For broadleaf trees, there are three different patterns, shown in the drawings. For conifers, there are four main patterns in which the needle or scale leaves grow, also shown in drawings.

There are lots of ways you can take a "snapshot" of your friend's leaves. You can make a leaf rubbing or a leaf print. You can press a leaf and save it whole. You can use a leaf from your tree as a stencil, or simply trace a leaf carefully to help you learn about and remember its shape. The drawings on pages 20 and 21 will show you how.

The best time to do any projects using leaves, especially for broadleaf trees, is in the fall, of course. That's when you will find lots of leaves on the ground that the tree won't need any more. If you want to use a leaf for a project any other time, you should take only a few leaves. After all, your friend needs those leaves to make food!

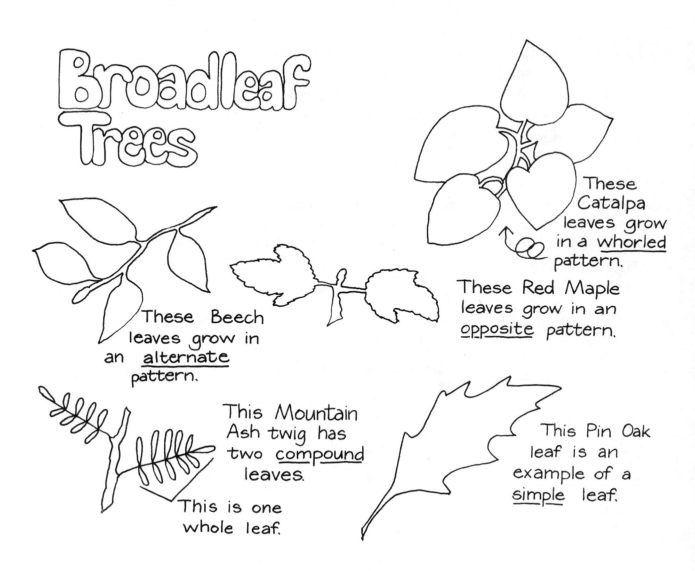

Broadleaf Trees

These Beech leaves grow in an alternate pattern.

These Catalpa leaves grow in a whorled pattern.

These Red Maple leaves grow in an opposite pattern.

This Mountain Ash twig has two compound leaves.

This is one whole leaf.

This Pin Oak leaf is an example of a simple leaf.

One final thought: Many people can identify a tree just by looking at its leaves. Maybe you already know what kind of tree your friend is, but if you don't and want to find out, libraries have lots of books that can help you. Often bringing just one leaf to a library is enough of a clue for you and a librarian to find your friend in a book.

Spring Leaves

Have you ever really watched what happens when spring wakes up a broadleaf tree? There is an easy way to watch buds grow into leaves.

If your tall green friend is a broadleaf tree, do this with your friend. If not, find a broadleaf tree if you can, so you can watch spring come close up.

Take a ribbon with you to your tree on a nice day in the very early spring. Look carefully at just one twig. Do you see any leaf buds?

Are they very tiny? Draw a picture of them. (Be sure to date your drawing.)

Tie the ribbon around your twig and return a few days later to look at the twig again. Date your drawing.

Do this as many times as you can, until the leaves are full grown.

Amazing!

Now you have "snapshots" of your tree at a very happy time in its life.

CONIFERS

Pines

Needles grow in bunches, and are "wrapped" at the base.

Firs

Needles are blunt at the end.

Spruce

Needles have four sides, and are sharp.

Some conifers have flat leaves that look like the scales on a fish. Red cedar is an example.

Different Kinds of Trees

hen someone says the word "tree," what do you picture in your mind? Draw the picture you have in your mind on a sheet of paper.

lot of people picture in their minds the kind of tree we call a **broadleaf** tree. "Broadleaf" is two words put together meaning "a leaf that is wide." **Deciduous** is another word for this kind of tree.

If you drew a tree that looks sort of like this, you drew a broadleaf tree. A broadleaf tree:

 Has leaves that look flat if you turn them on their edges, or broad (wide) if you look at them from the top;

 Needs lots of water for the three seasons it has leaves on it;

 Loses its leaves before cold weather; and

 Has no leaves in the cold season and survives almost without water, since its roots can't use frozen ice and snow.

Can you name a broadleaf tree?

hat would be the opposite of a "broadleaf"? "Narrowleaf" or "skinnyleaf"? There are trees with very narrow leaves, as skinny as needles. Can you guess what they are? Draw your guess on a sheet of paper.

If you drew a tree that looks like a Christmas tree, you drew the kind of tree we call a **conifer**.

A conifer:

 Grows its seeds inside cones (do you see the word "cone" inside the word "conifer"?);

 Keeps its leaves in wintertime;

 Loses and replaces its leaves a lot more gradually than a broadleaf; and

 Grows well in cold climates, because its leaves are so small and thick that they can catch the winter sun but won't lose important moisture.

18

ater, as you know, is very important to a plant. Have you ever wondered why we don't see saguaro cacti growing beside oak trees in Michigan? The answer is, they would drown!

A cactus living in the desert is used to storing very large amounts of water inside its thick spiny skin, to help it live through the very dry seasons of the desert. It would not know how to store the huge amounts of water from the ground further north and would die.

Water is also the reason why oak trees that love the wet up north can survive in Arizona only with the help of a friendly garden hose.

 alm trees are familiar to you especially if you live in Florida or California. They are different from other trees because:

 They *love* the heat. Even the almost tropical heat of California or Florida is a bit chilly for them;

 Most palms have a single trunk without true branches. Leaves grow directly from the trunk; and

 The main way they make more palm trees is through big central flowers (which many animals and people find really delicious—do you like bananas?).

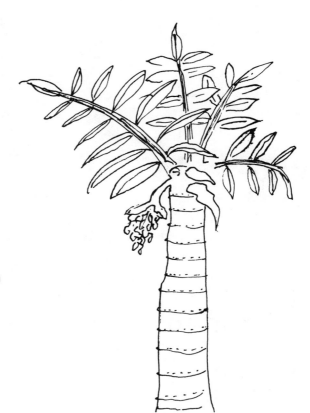

19

HOW TO KEEP A LEAF

Taking "snapshots" of your Tall Green Friend's leaves

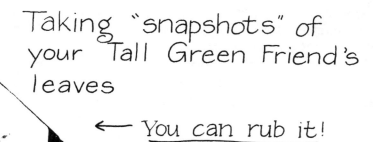

← You can rub it!
Put your leaf underneath some tracing paper on a flat surface. Using a crayon with the paper peeled off, rub over the place where the leaf is.

You can stencil it! →
Using a soft brush and tempera paint (available in toy stores and art supply stores), lay the leaf flat on the paper and brush away from the edge of the leaf. Hold the leaf edge gently as you go.

You can trace it! →

Hold the leaf gently with one hand. Trace around the edge, using a pencil, with the other hand.

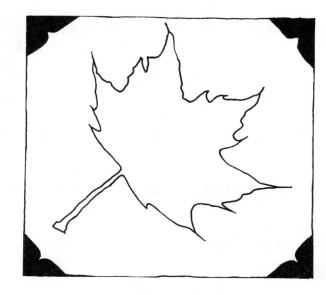

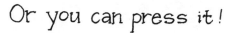

← You can print it!

Using a soft brush and tempera paint, cover the underside of your leaf with paint. Place it carefully, paint side down, on some paper on a kitchen counter or table. Cover it with a paper towel, and press it down with a rolling pin. Let the print dry. And be sure to clean up!

Or you can press it!

Take the biggest book you can find (or a stack of books). Sandwich your leaf in paper towels, press it between the pages, and wait two or three weeks. Then you can paste your leaf in your journal to save it.

Flowers, Fruit, and Seeds

In the spring, cherry trees bloom. Apple trees bloom. Crabapple, peach, and plum trees bloom. Did you know that maple trees bloom too? And on many city streets, sycamore trees (the kind of tree with the "camouflage" bark) bloom.

Flowers look like they bloom and then die, don't they? That is only partly true, because after the petals die, other parts of the flower stay on the tree. They grow and change and become fruit, if they belong on trees like maple or peach trees. Or they turn into nuts, like on pecan or hickory trees. Fruit and nuts are packages the tree makes to spread its seeds.

Sometimes trees make packages that don't look very edible to us, like pine cones or maple keys, but those packages still do good work in spreading their tree's seeds.

Lots of trees have flowers that aren't often noticed (except by bees), because they aren't colorful or fragrant. But here's a rule: If a tree has nuts or fruit in the fall, it had flowers in the spring.

- Did an oak tree with acorns blossom in the spring?
- Do you think *your* tree blossoms in the spring?

Actually, all trees grow some kind of flower. Young pine cones don't look like flowers, but they are. Catkins are another kind of flower. They often look like little bumpy "tails" at the ends of twigs. Alder trees, aspens, and birches are a few of the kinds of trees that have catkin flowers in the spring.

You may want to press your friend's flowers in a heavy book. Then, when they are dry, tape them carefully into your journal. Or you may want to draw your tree's flowers, fruit, or seeds.

Many Native Americans love the "tree people" and talk to them like friends. They learn about them by watching them year by year. They thank the tree people for the gifts they give to people, and they enjoy the beauty of the trees.

Maybe they know about a tree's language. Do you think you do?

A Coconut Climb

There are some delicious coconuts at the top of this tree. Climb up to get them by filling in the blanks on your own paper.

The numbers tell you how many letters there are in the answers. Answers can be found at the bottom of the page.

10. Air + water + (8) = tree food!

YUM!!!

9. "Skinnyleaf" could be another name for (7).

8. A tree's gift to you is (6).

7. You breathe out a gas called (13).

6. (9) leaves are wide and flat. Another name for "deciduous."

5. (11) is a sunlight trapper for green plants.

4. Before the fruits come the (7).

3. Chlorophyll makes most (6) green.

2. Sap carries (5) between roots and leaves.

1. Growing deep and spreading wide, (5) look for water.

WORD LIST

broadleaf	roots
flowers	oxygen
conifer	leaves
sunlight	sugar

chlorophyll
carbon dioxide

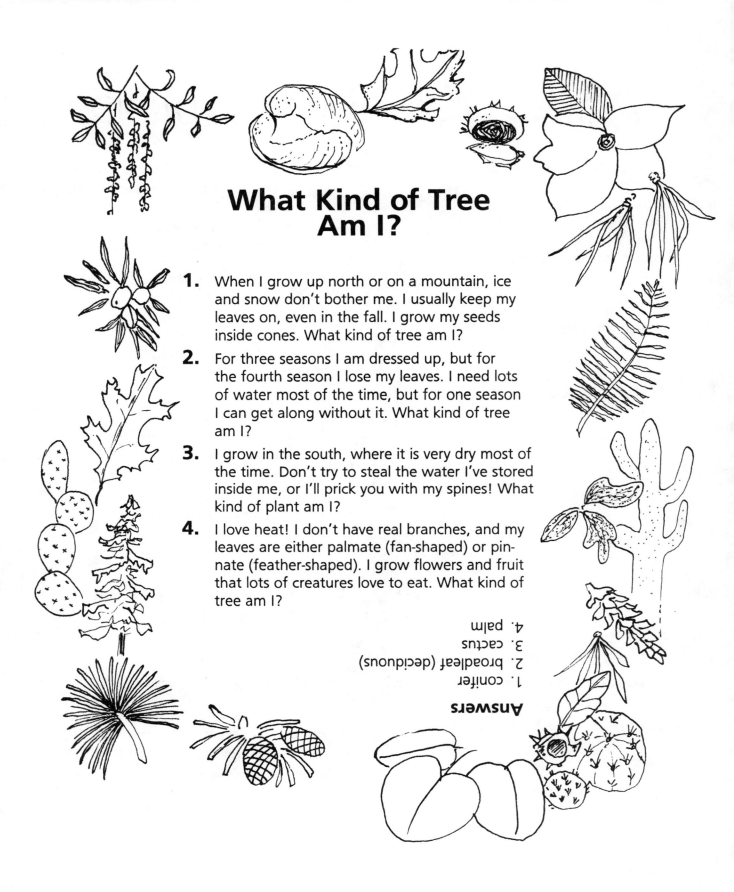

What Kind of Tree Am I?

1. When I grow up north or on a mountain, ice and snow don't bother me. I usually keep my leaves on, even in the fall. I grow my seeds inside cones. What kind of tree am I?

2. For three seasons I am dressed up, but for the fourth season I lose my leaves. I need lots of water most of the time, but for one season I can get along without it. What kind of tree am I?

3. I grow in the south, where it is very dry most of the time. Don't try to steal the water I've stored inside me, or I'll prick you with my spines! What kind of plant am I?

4. I love heat! I don't have real branches, and my leaves are either palmate (fan-shaped) or pinnate (feather-shaped). I grow flowers and fruit that lots of creatures love to eat. What kind of tree am I?

Answers

1. conifer
2. broadleaf (deciduous)
3. cactus
4. palm

CHAPTER 2

Green Plants

Here is a silly question: If there was only one plant in the world, what would it look like?

Take a piece of paper and draw this plant. Let your imagination run as wild as a wild horse in the spring. Fill that white space with stems and leaves and flowers. Draw the plant's roots if you want to.

Does your plant have one stem or a lot of them? Does it have toothed leaves like a dandelion or smooth leaves like a milkweed? Does it need thorns to keep animals from eating it? Does it have flowers? Does it have fruit?

Step Outside

Drawing a plant from your imagination gives you a chance to look at real plants differently. When you step outside, even in a city, you can see lots of different kinds of plants.

You can see moss growing on bricks, maybe, if you live in a place that gets lots of rain. Even in dry places, you can often see dandelions growing up in sidewalk cracks or clover growing up by gutters. Some plants just never give up. A tiny bit of soil, a little water from a street cleaner or someone's car washing, and up they grow. You can become an expert at finding tough plants that no one else notices in a city.

A tough plantain plant
grows in a city sidewalk crack.

In the country, you'll have a chance to see lots of different kinds of plants, too. You may have a garden, a field, or woods nearby. Just try to count all the different kinds of plants that grow near where you live sometime!

How are the plants you see in the real world like your imaginary plant?

Watching a Plant Grow Up

Maybe you have watched a plant grow from a seed to a grown-up plant. If you haven't and would like to, the drawing on page 28 will show you how to grow bean seeds.

Lots of seeds grow the same way bean seeds grow. Everything seems to happen all at once, doesn't it? The roots shoot down, looking for water and good things in the soil. At almost the same time, a stem and leaves shoot up toward the light, so that the tiny growing plant can begin to make its own food. (Chapter 1 can tell you how trees and all green plants do this.)

Soon, the roots of plants that are growing from seeds begin to look less like baby roots and more like the roots of a grown-up plant. The stem grows taller and stronger, so the plant can support more and more leaves.

When the plant is very small, it lives on food that was stored inside the seed. As the leaves grow, the plant can make food for itself.

Finally, the plant gets old enough to grow flowers and its own seeds. These seeds then get spread around to start more baby plants.

Flowers

Why are flowers important?

You probably have a favorite flower. Maybe it's your favorite because it's beautiful. Maybe it's your favorite because it smells good. Maybe it's your favorite because you know it will become a fruit that is good to eat. Or maybe you don't know why it is your favorite—it just is. Flowers are important to people for lots of reasons.

Flowers are important to plants because flowers are the beginnings of seeds which grow up into new plants. But many flowers need help to make seeds.

Growing Beans

You need:

- a drinking glass
- a few pinto beans
- water

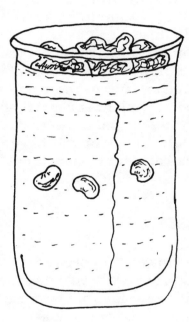

1. Fold a piece of paper towel so that it will be the same height as the glass. Line the glass with it.

2. Stuff the paper-towel-lined glass carefully with crumpled paper towels.

3. Drip some water slowly into the glass, so the paper towels get moist, but don't collapse with too much water.

4. Poke the beans between the side of the glass and the folded paper towel liner. Now you can watch the beans as they grow! Keep the paper towels moist, but not wet (too wet and your beans will rot).

When your beans get too big for the drinking glass, you can plant them in a pot or outside if the soil is warm enough.

Flowers, Bees, and Bats

You might know why bees and flowers go together. Did you know that each one gives the other the gift of life itself? The gift that flowers give to bees is food, the sweet **nectar**, for the bees and the young bees in the hive.

Bees give flowers the ability to make seeds.

How do they do that?

Pollination by an Insect or Animal

When the **stamens** are ripe, they burst open and the pollen grains are ready to leave the flower with the help of the pollinator who found the **nectaries**.

What happens to the pollen when it reaches another flower? If it is on the **stigma** (often stigmas are sticky, just so they can get pollen on them), the pollen grain grows a tube through the **style** into the **ovary**. Inside the ovary are the **ovules**, or tiny egg cells. The pollen and the ovules grow together, and the flower is pollinated.

The drawing doesn't have the pollen tube or the ovules labeled, but can you find them?

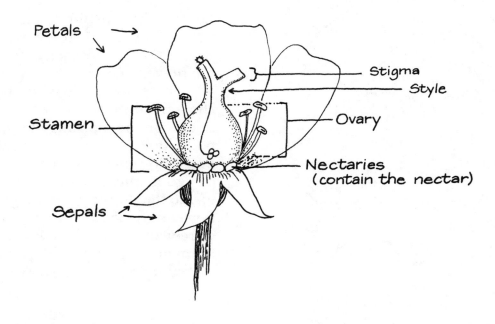

When you look at a flower closely, you can often see its pollen. It looks like a bright yellow dust. A bee or other insect flying from flower to flower looking for nectar scrapes off some of the flower's pollen onto its body. When it visits a different flower, the pollen gets scraped off onto that flower.

When the right kind of pollen gets to the right place on the right flower, that is called **pollination**. The drawing on page 29 can show you in more detail what happens when a flower gets pollinated.

Insects aren't the only creatures who are pollinators. Some kinds of cacti that grow in the desert look especially appealing to a certain kind of bat. Some kinds of plants have flowers that are shaped so bees can't get inside, but hummingbirds can. Bats and hummingbirds can be pollinators, too.

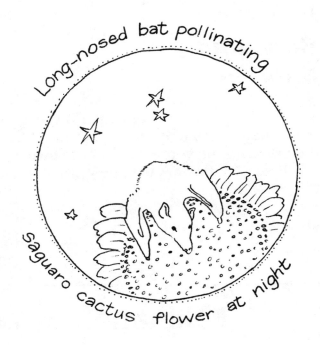

Long-nosed bat pollinating saguaro cactus flower at night

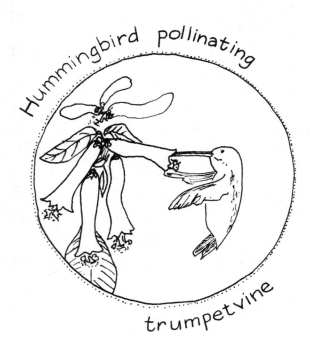

Hummingbird pollinating trumpet vine

Target: Nectar

Look at the drawing of the rhododendron flower on page 31. If you were a bee, would you know exactly where to go for the flower's nectar? How would you know?

Some flowers have spots, like the rhododendron flower. Some have faint lines, like the morning glory, to show the pollinator the way inside to the nectar. Some flowers are shaped so a pollinator can go in only one way. When they are inside the flower, they are guided by the flower's shape the way you would be if you were walking in a hallway with only one room at the end. Butter-and-eggs flowers and snapdragons are shaped that way.

A flower that looks like one big flower to us, like a daisy or a Queen Anne's Lace flower, may actually be lots of tiny flowers. All a pollinator has to do on this kind of flower is to step from one flower to the next, gathering the nectar (and shedding pollen). Sometimes you can watch bees moving on a daisy in a spiral pattern, starting at the outside and working toward the center.

Do you think you can learn something about how a flower is pollinated if you pretend you are a hungry bee the next time you look at it?

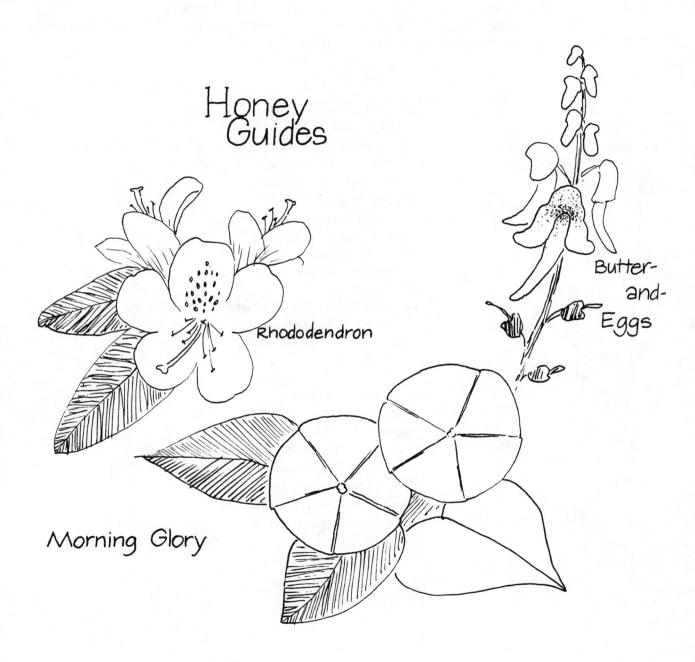

Honey Guides

Rhododendron

Butter-and-Eggs

Morning Glory

Wind

Some kinds of plants don't need pollinators at all to make seeds. They use the wind to spread their pollen. Their flowers are often very small and not at all colorful, so we usually don't notice them.

Grasses and many trees grow these kinds of flowers. Which kind of flower do you think would make more pollen, a bee-pollinated flower or a wind-pollinated flower? Here's a hint: If you were absolutely certain that your fragrance, color, and nectar were irresistible to a bee, would you go to a lot of trouble to make a lot of pollen?

Take a look at the drawings of different kinds of grasses. Do any of them live around you? Which parts of the grasses do you think are the flowers?

Fruit

Some kinds of fruit that we eat have only one seed inside them. Peaches are a kind of fruit with only one seed inside them. It's called a pit. Can you think of any other fruits with only one seed?

Some kinds of fruit have lots of seeds. Strawberries have lots of tiny seeds on the outside, right where you can see them. What about apples? Do apples have more than one seed inside them?

Whether fruit has lots of seeds inside or only one, the fruit part developed from the ovule of the flower.

32

The drawing on page 34 shows you how an apple flower becomes an apple. Even a tomato is a fruit!

The part of the apple that you eat tastes pretty good. Also, if you think about it, the tasty part protects the seeds inside. In fact, scientists use the word "fruit" to mean any part of a plant whose main job is to protect the seeds. So the "fruit" of a plant can be thin, like a pea pod, or thick and juicy, like an orange or an apple.

Seeds on the Move

Plants have roots and stay in one place all their lives, right? So when it comes time to send their seeds to the soil, so the seeds can grow in the spring, many plants have a problem. They don't want all their seeds to fall to the ground right around their own roots. If there were only one dandelion plant in the whole world and it came time to drop its seeds, what would happen if all the seeds ended up growing around the parent plant?

There would be only one small patch of dandelions in the whole world!

But you know what happens to a dandelion flower that has been visited by lots of bees and been pollinated. It closes up for a while, then opens again, this time with all those silky parachutes that the wind likes to play with. You might like to play with them, too.

When you blow on a full, ripe dandelion, you are helping the dandelion seeds go to places that don't have dandelions.

Did you know that when Europeans came to this country, they brought dandelions with them? Native Americans had never seen the plant before. The settlers carefully planted dandelions in their gardens, because they used them for medicine. But soon they no longer had to protect the dandelions in their gardens. Can you guess why?

You probably know of other plants that spread their seeds with the help of the wind.

Yum, Delicious!

A wild blackberry hanging on a bush, fat and gleaming, looks very good to many people, animals, and birds. We may not stop to notice the seeds inside!

Some seeds are wrapped in fruit packages that birds and animals find delicious. That's another way that plants spread their seeds. Lots of seeds can pass right through animals after they have eaten them. Have you ever seen bird droppings with seeds inside them? If those seeds land in the right place, up they will sprout!

You probably know how delicious raspberries, blueberries, and blackberries can be, even if you have tasted only store-bought ones. Many animals feel the same way when they find them growing wild. The fruit is squishy and delicious, but the seeds are hard and can't be digested. Eventually, the seeds end up outside an animal's body again, in a raccoon's, or a bear's, or a fox's droppings, to sprout up in the spring. The plant does the bird or the animal the favor of growing some delicious fruit. The bird or the animal does the plant the favor of spreading its seeds.

How an apple flower becomes an apple

1. The ovaries of the flower are contained in the <u>receptacle</u> that looks like part of a flower's stem. Inside the ovaries are the ovules, or future seeds. The drawing shows what you might see if you cut the flower in half. (See "Parts of a flower" for more about flower structure.)

Receptacle

2. The flower is pollinated by a honeybee. The petals die and fall off. What's left?

3. The ovary, containing the seeds. It gets bigger...

4. ... and bigger...

5. PLOP!

Many flowering plants grow fruit and seeds in their own ways. How does a zucchini, thistle, or dandelion flower become "fruit"?

Explosions

Some plants have solved the seed transportation problem in a mighty explosive way. Their seeds ripen inside a thin case that gets more and more dry in the sun and the wind. One day, the wind blows a leaf against them, or an animal brushes against them, or you go out for a walk and touch them with just your fingertip, and BOOM! That seed pod explodes! Seeds can go surprisingly great distances that way.

There is a wild plant called jewelweed whose seed pods explode that way. The plant is also called "touch-me-not." Can you guess why?

Hitching a Ride

There's another way plants get animals to spread their seeds. Have you ever picked burdocks from a dog's fur? Or maybe from your socks?

Lots of plants have seeds that stick, stick, stick to any animal's fur that just passes by. Or to your pants or socks, if you just brush against them.

Then the little seeds have a chance to find a new home far away from their parents. But they have to find the right place to grow.

Burdock People

Burdock plants grow in many parts of the country. They like roadsides, old fields, and maybe the edges of parking lots. You may first notice them when they bloom—they have spikey-looking flowers and prickly-looking leaves.

You can collect their seeds in the fall on your pants, socks, or sweaters. Your dog or cat can collect them, too. The seeds are easy to collect without even knowing you're collecting them!

You can also collect burdock seeds to stick together. You can make burdock people, animals, or anything that comes to mind.

When you're finished with the burdock seeds, just return them to the place you found them, so new burdocks can grow next year.

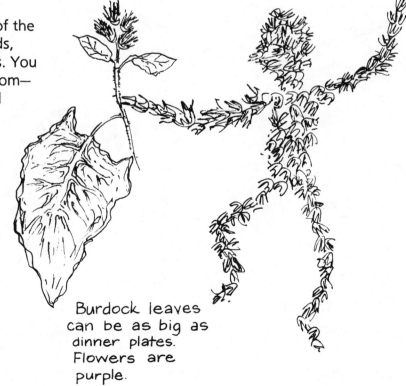

Burdock leaves can be as big as dinner plates. Flowers are purple.

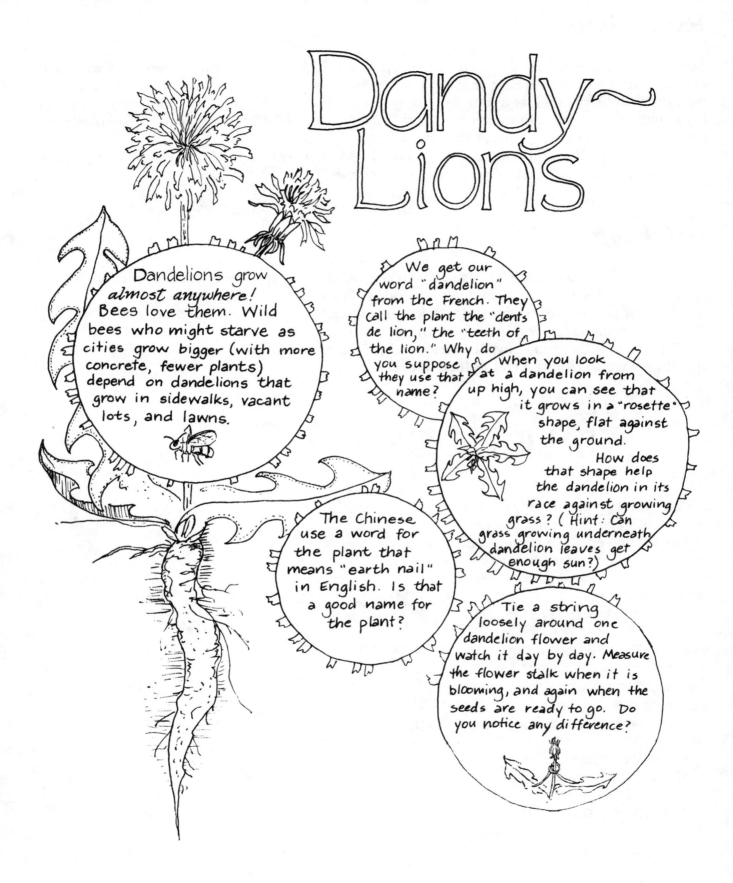

Dandy~ Lions

Dandelions grow *almost anywhere!* Bees love them. Wild bees who might starve as cities grow bigger (with more concrete, fewer plants) depend on dandelions that grow in sidewalks, vacant lots, and lawns.

We get our word "dandelion" from the French. They call the plant the "dents de lion," the "teeth of the lion." Why do you suppose they use that name?

When you look at a dandelion from up high, you can see that it grows in a "rosette" shape, flat against the ground.

How does that shape help the dandelion in its race against growing grass? (Hint: Can grass growing underneath dandelion leaves get enough sun?)

The Chinese use a word for the plant that means "earth nail" in English. Is that a good name for the plant?

Tie a string loosely around one dandelion flower and watch it day by day. Measure the flower stalk when it is blooming, and again when the seeds are ready to go. Do you notice any difference?

Where Plants Grow

All plants will only grow in the places that are right for them. Those places may not look very special to you, but the more you learn about plants, the more you can see how each plant you look at has found a special place to live.

Try this: Think about places near where you live that are very different from each other. A pond and a dry sunny yard are an example. A field and some woods are another example. If you live in a city, a park with a playing field and shade trees can give you enough contrast to see the differences in the plants that grow in each place.

- Do plants growing in shade have bigger leaves than plants growing in the sun?
- Do plants growing in a dry place look somehow tougher than plants that grow in a pond?

Even if you can't find two different places to look at where you live, you can see really big differences just by looking through any book about plants. Does a water lily in a photograph look like it's made of half water? Does a desert plant like a mesquite tree look tough, like it has to fight for every drop of water?

Adaptation

The reason there isn't just one plant in the world is because there isn't just one environment. There are places where it is hot all the time and places where it is cold all the time, and lots of places in between.

There are places where there is a lot of water for plants, animals, and people, and places where there isn't much at all. And lots of places in between.

Different environments are good for different kinds of plants. Do you remember the drawing of the oak tree and the cactus on page 19? The cactus is **adapted** to the desert because it can store large amounts of water inside itself for dry times on the desert. (And it can protect that water with its prickly spines!)

You can learn more about the ways plants can adapt by putting yourself in their places.

Grapevines, for instance, grow in the same kinds of soil and

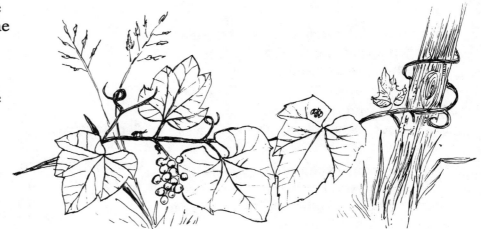

sunny places that many other plants also grow in. Grapevines compete for sunlight with all of these plants. Grapevines have weak stems and can't hold themselves upright to get the sun on their leaves, which they need to make their food. What a problem! Grapevines can't grow taller than other plants to get to the sun, so what do they do? They grow very fast and send out tendrils to wind around other plants, fences, and trees to hoist themselves up into the sun.

Leaves and Sun

How does each leaf on a plant get the most possible sunlight?

An Experiment

You need:

- a pencil
- paper "leaves"
- tape
- a flashlight

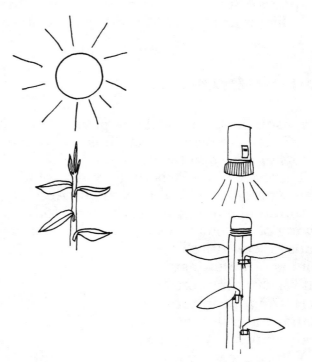

How to do it:

1. Cut out ten leaf shapes with one-inch "stems."

2. Go outside and carefully observe the leaf arrangement on the stem of a plant. Tape your leaves onto the pencil in exactly the same way.

3. Go indoors and shine the flashlight on top of your "pencil plant." Do any leaves shade the ones underneath?

4. Now you can play around with your "leaves." Can you figure out other ways to arrange them so that each leaf gets all the sun it possibly can? Can you find these arrangements on real plants outside?

A question:

Generally speaking, which plants have *bigger* leaves—plants that grow in the sun or plants that grow in the shade? (*Hint*: All green plants need the sun to make their own food. Shade plants need to "gather" about as much light to make food as sun plants do.)

Problems and Solutions

In adapting to different growing conditions, plants have developed different ways to solve specific problems. Do insects love to munch on leaves? One way plants keep insect munching to a minimum is by making chemicals that make leaves taste bad to a bug. Or plants can grow more leaves than they need for survival. That way, if insects eat a few, there are still plenty of leaves left to make their food.

Do animals eat plants? Some plants grow thorns to keep animals away. Grasses grow well even in pastures where cows eat them because they can grow quickly right back up from their roots even after they have been eaten.

Water is a difficult place for plants with stems and roots to grow. Plants that live in water have lots of ways to solve the problem of the distance between where the roots grow (the soil at the bottom of the lake, stream, or pond) and where the sunlight is (at the surface of the water). The simplest way to solve the problem is to grow a very long stem, then grow leaves at the top of the stem at the water's surface where they can collect the light.

Wildflower Seeds for Your Garden

You can buy wildflower seeds, but why not collect them yourself? When you go for a walk, take a handful of bright yellow or red ribbon to tie around plants you might like to bring to your garden. Then you can find them again to collect a few of their seeds when they are dry and ripe. Be sure to leave plenty of seeds for birds and animals to eat. And be sure to sprinkle some seeds around so the plant will grow next year in the same place.

How to Hunt a Plant

We have many things to learn about why plants grow the way they do. Scientists use a lot of expensive equipment to learn plant secrets. It seems they can never come to the end of learning about even the smallest plants.

But you can learn a lot about any plant you choose. All you have to do is hunt it! The nice thing about hunting plants instead of animals is that plants stay still.

Why not choose a plant and sit down to watch it just as you might watch an animal? "Fawn Magic" (page 83) in Chapter 4 will give you some ideas about how to stay comfortable as you "hunt."

Make yourself really comfortable and watch the plant. Plan to spend lots of time, and bring drawing materials and a ribbon.

The best way to hunt a plant is to draw it as carefully as you can. Draw the plant well enough so that someone looking at your drawing would be able to recognize your plant if you took him or her to the area where it grows.

Chances are that you have seen
Trifolium, with leaves of green.
In groups of three my leaves may grow.
Or maybe four, for luck, you know.

My flowers can be white or red.
They make fine honey, it is said.
Bees love me, and horses too.
They know me well. Do you?

Gather a bunch of
trifolium flowers
together for a
good smell.

Answer: Clover! "Tri" means "three" and "folium" means "leaf" in Latin. Red or white clover grows with three leaves to a stem.

As you draw your plant, you will be able to see if any insect is munching on it. Some plants have chemicals inside them that bugs don't like to eat, so those plants are left alone. But many plants can't get through a season without bugs nibbling at them. Normally, the plant grows just fine in spite of the nibbles.

- Do any bees come to visit your plant?
- Do any birds come to eat your plant's seeds?

Can you tell from your drawing what time of year it is? You can often tell if it's spring, summer, fall, or winter by the size of the plant; whether it has buds, flowers, or seeds; and what shade of green it is. (Usually, in spring, plants are a light green. They get darker as they get older.)

You can't really draw accurately the kind of soil in which your plant grows. But that is important, too. How about describing the place where you found your plant in words—"field," or "woods," or "by the pond"—at the bottom of your drawing? Each place has a different kind of soil.

When you finish the drawing, date it. Then tie the ribbon loosely around the plant as a marker so you can return to it later. Throughout its life it will grow and change a lot. You may want to make more drawings. Date them too, so you can compare them.

Plants and People

You learned in Chapter 1 how trees and other green plants give us the oxygen we need to breathe. And you know how all the food we eat, even if it is not itself a plant, comes from plants.

You probably know where the clothes we wear come from. Even man-made fabric, like polyester, comes from oil, which was once plant material long ago.

Many plants that don't seem important can be very useful to people. Quinine, a medicine that comes from a tropical plant, has saved many people from a tropical disease called malaria. For centuries, people have been using a flowering plant called foxglove to make a heart medicine. Some people who make old-fashioned medicines from plants say that for every disease, there is a cure that can be found in the plant kingdom.

What Is a Weed?

Some people say that "a weed is any plant that is in a place where you don't want it." Plants like pricker bushes, poison ivy, thistles, and crab grass can find their way into places that are certainly inconvenient for us. But we may want to stop and think before we wish that those plants would somehow vanish from the face of the earth.

It may help you to know, even if you have a bad case of poison ivy, that the same plant that caused you such misery will also feed many birds with its berries in the fall.

Leaves of three, Let them be!

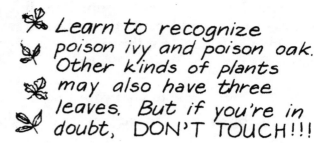 Learn to recognize poison ivy and poison oak. Other kinds of plants may also have three leaves. But if you're in doubt, DON'T TOUCH!!!

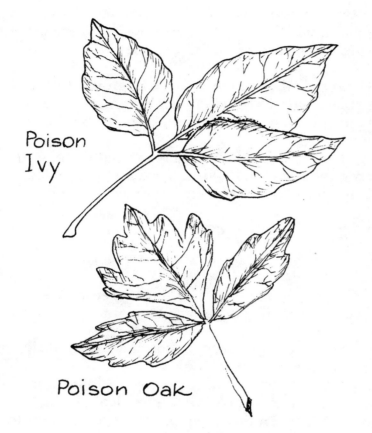

Poison Ivy

Poison Oak

Poison ivy, poison oak, and poison sumac are well named, even though you would never eat them. They have a resin, or sap, that you can't see but certainly can feel a little while after it gets on your hands. The resin irritates your skin and makes you itch.

Wash your hands quickly and carefully if you think you have touched any of these plants.

And don't forget poison sumac!

Poison sumac has white berries. Other sumacs have red berries.

Collecting
tiny flowers

ANYBODY can collect BIG flowers and arrange them in a BIG vase. But it takes a sharp eye to see and appreciate the tiny flowers you can find almost anywhere, even on a playground.

AND it takes a good imagination to find the right tiny vases for those flowers.

DO YOU have sharp eyes and a good imagination?

The Adaptation Game

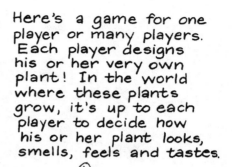

Here's a game for one player or many players. Each player designs his or her very own plant! In the world where these plants grow, it's up to each player to decide how his or her plant looks, smells, feels and tastes.

HOW TO PLAY

You need: one die, paper, and something to draw with

Each player rolls the die once per turn. Each player will roll the die a total of four times, once for each of the four game boxes. If you are the only player, roll the die four times, once for each of the four game boxes.

As you go through the game boxes, think about what your plant will look like. For example, if you roll "desert" in game box #1, you can start to think about what you know about desert plants. They need to save water, so their leaves are tiny or spiny to prevent evaporation. Game box #2 will give you some ideas about what kind of defenses the plant may need to avoid being eaten. Game box #3 will give you a clue about what your plant's flowers will look like, and game box #4 will help you decide what its fruit or seeds will look like.

When you get to game box #4, draw your plant. Show everyone your plant and talk about it, because

☙ YOU MADE IT! ❧

Don't forget to give your plant a really good name.

AN EXAMPLE

Here is what a 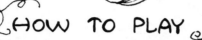 might look like.

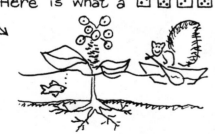

The squirreltail plant grows in ponds. Its stem is very very hairy. Not many needle-nosed bugs can get through all that hair! There are lots of tiny white flowers that smell bad, but flies love. Squirrels come in boats in the fall to collect the berries. They bury them in the mud and forget they're there!

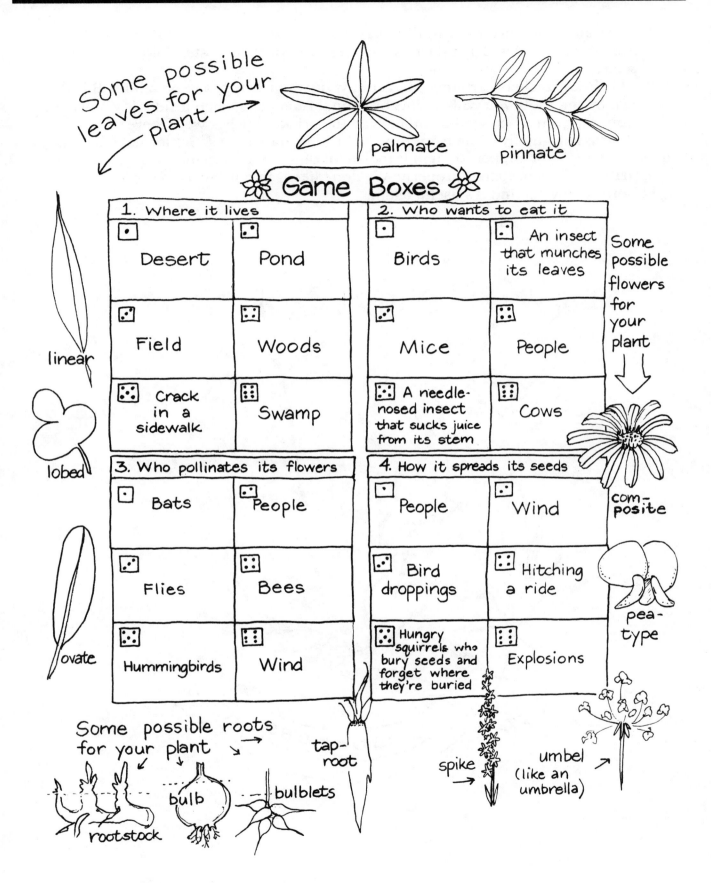

Some possible leaves for your plant →

palmate

pinnate

linear

lobed

ovate

Game Boxes

1. Where it lives

⚀ Desert	⚁ Pond
⚂ Field	⚃ Woods
⚄ Crack in a sidewalk	⚅ Swamp

2. Who wants to eat it

⚀ Birds	⚁ An insect that munches its leaves
⚂ Mice	⚃ People
⚄ A needle-nosed insect that sucks juice from its stem	⚅ Cows

3. Who pollinates its flowers

⚀ Bats	⚁ People
⚂ Flies	⚃ Bees
⚄ Hummingbirds	⚅ Wind

4. How it spreads its seeds

⚀ People	⚁ Wind
⚂ Bird droppings	⚃ Hitching a ride
⚄ Hungry squirrels who bury seeds and forget where they're buried	⚅ Explosions

Some possible flowers for your plant ⇩

composite

pea-type

Some possible roots for your plant ↘

rootstock

bulb

bulblets

tap-root

spike

umbel (like an umbrella) ↗

Thistles are so important to goldfinches that they wait until long after other birds have raised their families. Then they use thistledown for their nests. Goldfinches also eat thistle seeds.

Prickly briar thickets certainly can get in your way when you're on a hike. But if you look down by the roots you will see lots of animal runs going deep inside. If you were a rabbit running from a fox, would you be glad the pricker bushes were there?

Crab grass originally came from Europe just like dandelions. Settlers called crab grass "millet" and ate it for supper, though it took a lot of work to prepare. Crab grass seed is very nutritious if it's prepared properly. We don't like it in our lawns, but who knows? Maybe some day we'll find it's useful again.

CHAPTER 3

Soil

Have you ever wondered about the ground you're standing on or what the building you're in is built upon? "Just dirt," right? Usually we take it for granted. We even use the word "dirt" to mean something bad. If your face is dirty, it usually means you have to wash the dirt off to get clean.

In a way, it's a shame that we often use the word "dirt" to mean something bad. In this book, dirt, or soil, gets a whole chapter to itself, because all of life on earth depends on the goodness of the soil. If the soil is healthy, we are healthy.

How can soil be healthy? It's just dirt. If you hold soil in your hand, it feels lumpy, or sandy, wet, dry, dusty, cold, or crumbly. Maybe you'll find an earthworm or a grub in a handful of soil. Is the soil you hold in your hand healthy?

Healthy soil isn't dead. Parts of it are alive! Mostly with creatures and plants you can't see. You can tell if soil is healthy and alive, though, by looking at what grows from it. Do the plants growing in it look healthy? If they do, the soil is healthy too.

Healthy Soil Grows Healthy People

If soil is healthy, it grows healthy plants. People need healthy plants to eat. Perhaps when you go to the grocery store, your mom or dad teaches you how to choose the best oranges, celery, or lettuce.

You know what good vegetables or fruit look like and taste like, and certainly you know these things grow from healthy soil. There are other things that you eat that grow from soil, too, though they don't look like fruit or vegetables.

Bread is made from flour. Flour is ground wheat. Wheat is a grass plant that farmers grow in big fields. Each spring, farmers look carefully at the soil in their fields to find out how healthy it is, to see if they need to enrich the soil or plant special crops that will make the soil healthier.

Even if you eat meat, the meat you eat depends on healthy soil. Hamburger meat, for example, comes from cattle. Cattle eat plants, grass mostly. And grass, of course, needs good soil to grow.

Everything on earth that lives depends on soil for food. Is soil just one kind of thing, or lots of different things all mixed together?

Think Big, Think Tiny

We can learn what the soil is made of. To learn about soil, we have to do two things with our minds.

The first is to think very big thoughts, thoughts about mountains grinding against each other and ocean waves pounding against cliffs. Rocks are pounded into tiny pieces in lots of ways. Those tiny pieces of rock are a very important part of soil.

The second kind of thinking you have to do to understand how soil is made is to think very tiny thoughts. The tiny pieces of rock become food for a special kind of plant called a lichen. Lichens break the rock down into even tinier pieces with plant juices. When the lichens die, the dead plants mix in with the tiny pieces of rock. Bigger plants can grow on the soil that has been made by the lichens.

All of this happens in a tiny space over a long time, so it is impossible to see bare rock turn into a forest in one lifetime. But over many lifetimes, that is what happens.

So when you picture the making of soil in your mind, you have to think really big and then think really tiny.

Thinking Big

Imagine two boulders rolling down a hill, bashing into each other, breaking off pieces of rock from each other.

Imagine waves in an ocean or a lake coming into shore, picking up billions and billions of pebbles and stones, and throwing them against each other. Have you ever noticed how smooth the pebbles are? Now you know why. Rolling around in the water, the pebbles rub and chip each other. The rubbings and chippings eventually become sand or soil.

To think big about soil you have to think big about time, too. Have you ever been to a graveyard? Tombstones that were made recently have letters that are very easy to read. They are as clear and crisp as the letters on this page.

But the gravestones of the people who lived at the time your grandparents were children may be harder to read. And gravestones from the time of the Declaration of Independence may be impossible to read!

That is because of something called **weathering**. That's when rain, ice, and snow wear down anything that is out in the weather. The tiny particles of stone in the tombstone that made letters easy to read 200 years ago have weathered away, and perhaps became part of the soil that, along with other things, grew the apple that you ate for lunch yesterday!

Thinking Tiny

When you hold a handful of soil, you are holding lots of tiny things mixed together. Some of them may be living— small, but still big enough for you to see, like a mushroom, an ant, or a bit of root. Some of them may be alive but far too tiny for a human eye to see without a microscope, like a fungus spore or the tiny plants that give soil that rich smell.

And some of the tiny things that are a part of soil may not be alive. They may be small but still big enough for us to see, like grains of sand, sticks, or bits of dead leaves. Or they may be too small for us to see, like tiny bits of clay or rock dust.

All these things can be a part of soil.

Fungus and Bacteria

When a tree or a plant dies, it becomes part of the soil, which can take many, many years. (In warm rain forests, it takes much less time.) A tree or other plant can become part of the soil only with the help of small living things, many of them so small that you can't see them.

Think about this: The world might be full of dead trees and animals too if it weren't for the tiny bacteria and fungi that we mostly can't see. We call the work they do the **process of decay.**

Bacteria are too small to see with our eyes alone. To see bacteria, we need microscopes.

A Sandpaper Experiment

You can help your mind to think big about soil by performing this experiment.

You need:

- two hard wooden or plastic blocks that you can hold comfortably in each hand
- two pieces of sandpaper
- a sheet of white paper

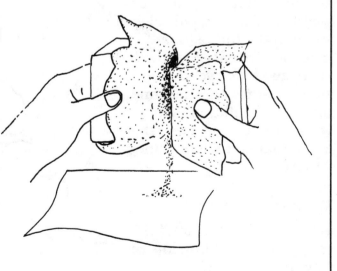

Place the white paper in front of you. Wrap the two pieces of sandpaper firmly around the blocks. Now rub the two surfaces together.

What do you see starting to collect on the white paper?

You may have heard that bacteria cause all kinds of diseases. That is true. But there are many kinds of bacteria and some kinds are very important to the health of the soil.

One bacterium alone is very tiny and doesn't do much. But when bacteria find good places to live, they grow very quickly—one bacterium can split into two bacteria, and those two can split into four bacteria, then eight, and so on. One bacterium can become millions of bacteria very quickly, when it finds what it needs to grow. So in a handful of soil there may be huge numbers of bacteria growing.

Bacteria eat the dead bodies of things that were once alive. They eat dead plants, dead trees, and dead animals. When the bacteria die themselves, the goodness that was in the dead things they ate becomes part of the goodness of the soil. Bacteria turn dead things into healthy soil.

Fungus is a living thing that eats dead plant material. But it is neither a plant nor an animal. Scientists give fungi a whole kingdom to themselves. Some fungus is big enough for you to see. Have you ever seen a mushroom on a log? Or mold on a piece of bread? Mushrooms and other fungi can't make their own food, so they take their food from plants that have died. They slowly help the dead plants and animals become part of the soil so new plants can grow.

The new plants that grow may be food for animals. And some of these plants and animals will be food for people.

How to draw a mushroom
so it looks like it's
R E A L !

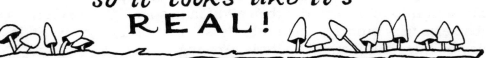

1. Find a mushroom.

2. Notice its shape. Is it TALL AND SKINNY or short and plump? All mushrooms are different.

3. Mushroom caps can be:

convex,   bell-shaped, or   conical (cone-shaped).

   Which one is yours? Draw your mushroom's shape.

4. Can you see the bottom of your mushroom's cap? If you can, here is how to draw it.

Draw the top shape and stem first. See how the cap goes up in the middle?

Draw the underside from left to right. Stop at the stem, lift up your pencil, and continue.

Shade the bottom of the cap, because there is a shadow there!

WARNING! Do not touch or eat mushrooms!

The Great Circle

The plants that send their roots down into the soil take what they need from the soil and turn it into roots, stems, leaves, and flowers. That is why, when a plant dies, fungi and bacteria are needed to eat dead plants and return the goodness in the plant to the soil. Bacteria return the goodness in dead animals to the soil. What was a dead plant or animal becomes nutrients (a kind of "food") for new plants.

So plants take nutrients from the soil. Animals take nutrients from the plants that got nutrients from the soil. The goodness of the nutrients is returned to the soil after the plant's or the animal's death, but only with the help of bacteria and fungi, through the process of decay.

A tree dies and falls to the ground.

Soon, carpenter ants build a nest inside the fallen tree. Bracket fungus takes hold. A rabbit discovers the log has become hollow enough to make a home.

Many plants and animals that are so tiny you can't see them get to work too. They eat up the old wood, die, and add their bodies to the soil. After many years, the old log is unrecognizable. It has become a part of the soil.

A bird flies over the patch of soil, dropping a maple tree seed. A sapling tree grows up exactly where the old tree died many years before.

53

SPROUTS

Here is one way to grow some surprise plants. For this project, you will need some sterile soil—soil that will not grow anything on its own. Ask an adult to help you bake two to three cups of soil in your oven for 1 $\frac{1}{2}$ hours at 350 degrees.

Now you can see what you brought home in your shoes!

■ Scrape the mud off your shoes after you've walked through a field or the woods on a wet day, mix it with a little water, and leave it overnight to soak.

■ The next day, put some sterile soil in a container, spread your mud on top, and cover the whole thing with plastic wrap. Keep it moist but not wet and wait a few weeks. What happens?

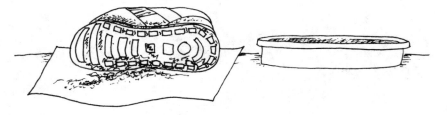

Animals and Soil

Many animals help make soil and keep it good for growing. Some of them are familiar to us, like woodchucks. The burrows that woodchucks make are very important, in an odd kind of way. Many plants love soil that has a lot of air between the crumbs of dirt. Woodchucks' burrows collapse with time, and what was a burrow becomes soil with lots of air mixed in.

Earthworms do the same thing. They eat their way through soil, leaving a tunnel behind them. They do something else that is very important, too. The soil they eat is

air into the soil and they grind up the soil into finer pieces as they eat. The tinier the particles of soil are, the easier it is for plants to use them.

Some farmers buy earthworms to help make their soil richer!

ground up very fine as they eat it. Sometimes you can see the **castings** they leave behind, at the entrance to a worm tunnel. Castings look like wet mounds of coiled string. They come from the insides of worms.

Worms help make the soil much better for plants in two ways: They bring

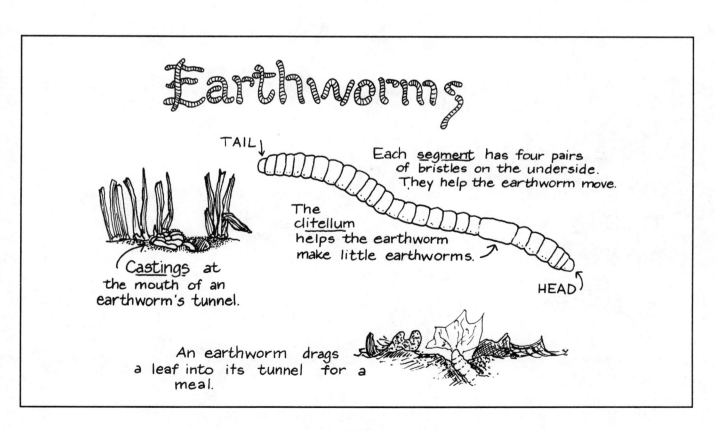

Earthworms

TAIL

Each <u>segment</u> has four pairs of bristles on the underside. They help the earthworm move.

The <u>clitellum</u> helps the earthworm make little earthworms.

HEAD

<u>Castings</u> at the mouth of an earthworm's tunnel.

An earthworm drags a leaf into its tunnel for a meal.

Insects in Soil

Can you name some insects that you are likely to find in a spadeful of soil? There's a very good chance that if you name even one insect, the insect you name spends all or part of its life in the soil. Most of the more than a million kinds of insects do.

In a spadeful of dirt, you may find insects that live in the soil or are just passing through the spadeful of dirt on their way to somewhere else. They include:

- ants
- beetles
- aphids
- fly pupae (Pupae are insects that haven't grown up yet.)
- beetle pupae

These are the kinds of insects you may find. If you let the list include animals that aren't actually insects because they have more than six legs, you may find:

- wireworms
- centipedes
- millipedes
- spiders
- mites
- springtails
- sow bugs

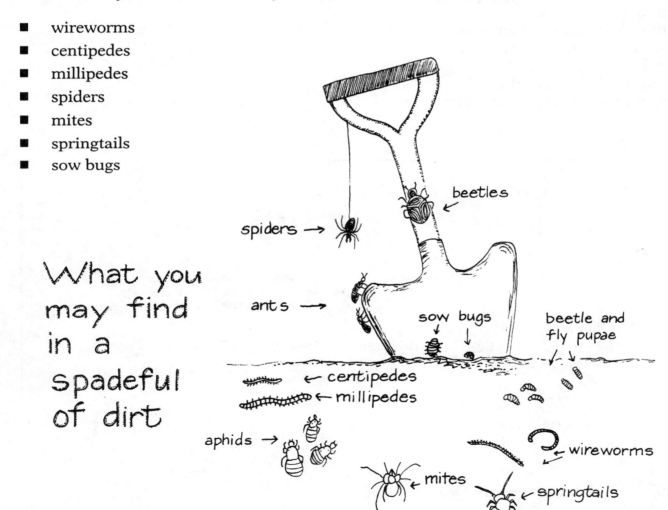

What you may find in a spadeful of dirt

Nematodes and Protozoa

Nematodes are very tiny animals. You can picture them in your mind as very tiny eels that move in and out among the roots of plants. They are so tiny that 50 nematodes would fit end to end in one inch. They may eat bacteria in the soil, if they are very small, or each other, if they are slightly larger. Sometimes they suck juices from plant roots and may kill the plants.

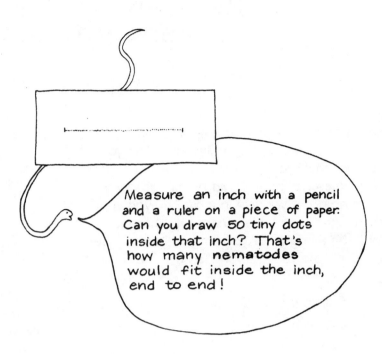

Measure an inch with a pencil and a ruler on a piece of paper. Can you draw 50 tiny dots inside that inch? That's how many **nematodes** would fit inside the inch, end to end!

Tiniest of all are the **protozoa**. Scientists have decided that protozoa are neither plants nor animals. Some protozoa are able to live as plants do, getting their energy from sunlight. But sometimes, when they are in the dark, they behave more like fungi, absorbing food into their bodies from their surroundings. They swim along in the water between bits of soil. The two main kinds of protozoa are **amebas**, which constantly change their shapes to move, and **flagellates**, which move with the help of a kind of whip on the ends of their bodies.

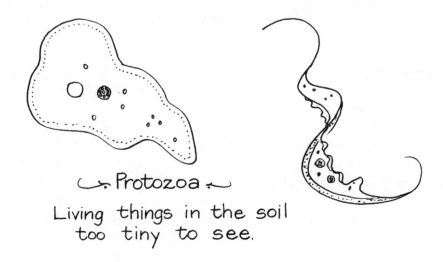

Protozoa
Living things in the soil too tiny to see.

How Can You See the World Beneath Your Feet?

The simplest way you can begin to learn about soil and the creatures that live in it is to go to your own backyard. Ask your parents to show you a place where it would be all right to do a little digging. If you live in a city, maybe your parents know about a vacant lot where it would be all right for you to dig. Don't forget that parks are for everyone, so don't dig there!

You need:
- old clothes
- a bucket of water
- a foot-long ruler
- four pencils
- some ribbon or twine
- a trowel
- big pieces of white paper or some newspaper

You will want to choose a time to do this project when the soil will be easy to work. When it is very dry, it can be as hard as cement, so try to do this after a rainfall or after watering. You will want the soil to be moist, but not muddy.

Become a Soil Scientist

Wear old clothes when you do this, so you won't have to worry about getting dirty.

You will be digging out about a one-foot (30-centimeter) square section of earth. You don't have to make your hole exactly square, but to help you keep your hole about the right size, use your four pencils and twine or ribbon as shown in the drawing.

Next, use your trowel to dig slowly and carefully. How is what you're doing different from digging any old hole? The difference is, you are a *scientist* now. You are digging into the soil to see if you can learn what soil is. So go slowly!

Take a clump of grass or weeds that you have just dug up and look at the roots. Are there any living creatures you can see among the roots? If there are, remove them carefully after taking a look at them, because the next step is to swish the roots around in your bucket of water. What do the roots look like after the soil is washed away? How long do you think the roots would be if you laid them end to end? One scientist spent a lot of time estimating that all the roots of a four-month-old rye plant (a kind of grass), placed end to end, would be over 7,000 miles (11,2000 kilometers) long!

Feel, Smell, Look

Spend a lot of time feeling the soil and smelling it too. Good farmers can learn a lot just by doing these two things; then they can plan the best way to use their soil. Does your soil smell good?

Is your soil hard to crumble between your fingers? If so, there may be a lot of clay in your soil. Is it gritty? Maybe there's a lot of sand there. Is it light and crumbly? Maybe you are holding the kind of soil many plants love to grow in.

Dig down a few inches. What do you find? You are a scientist, so classify what you find. Place living things on one piece of paper and nonliving things on the other. Part of the fun is deciding for yourself what is "living" and what is not. Is a broken-off twig a living thing? Is an insect's wing? Don't worry about being right or wrong. Deciding whether something is living or nonliving is just your own private brain-teaser. Try to name everything you find, too, although that may not always be easy. As you now know, scientists don't always find that an easy job either.

As you dig, do you see different layers in the soil? If you live in a recently built house, you may not see many layers because the people who built your house often scrape the topsoil from the places where they build. It may be many years before you see the different layers that you can find in a place where the soil hasn't been disturbed for a while.

Clean Up

After you are finished, don't forget to clean up. Try to leave your place as much the way you found it as possible. Press the soil back into the hole, put the plants back on top, and pour the water from the bucket on top of your square foot, slowly, to help settle the grains of soil and give the plants' roots a chance to start growing again. And, of course, give the living creatures a chance to return to their homes!

When you were working, you may have turned up some sow bugs. Page 60 has a drawing of a sow bug and shows a way you can see how a sow bug helps make soil.

Sow Bugs

Chances are good that if you've poked around under logs or picked up stones you have seen some sow bugs. They look like this:

Or like this, if they feel threatened:

You can see how sow bugs help make soil.

You need:

- two covered jars with air holes
- 8 to 10 sow bugs
- plenty of plant material from the place where you found the sow bugs

Place the sow bugs gently inside jar #1, along with half of the plant material. In jar #2, put the other half of the plant material, but no sow bugs. Keep the jars out of direct sunlight and keep everything moist.

What starts to happen after a few days?

When you are done, be sure to return the sow bugs to their homes.

S.O.S.—Save Our Soil

There are countries in the world where people have farmed the same soil for thousands of years. That soil has grown the food to feed children in those countries who are your own age. It feeds their parents and their grandparents. The same soil grew the plants that their great-grandparents ate, and their great-grandparents' parents, and generations before them.

Why is that important?

It is important because it is too easy to lose the soil. It can be lost through **erosion**, when rain washes soil away from fields. You can see how powerful even raindrops can be by doing the experiment on page 61.

Soil can be lost through the use of some kinds of farming tools and techniques. Farmers can plow their land in ways that keep the soil in its place, or they can plow carelessly, so soil is washed away with the rain. Heavy machinery can press down on the soil so that the air that roots need is pressed out of the soil. If soil washes away or becomes useless, people may go hungry.

But there are ways that even worn-out soil can begin to grow plants to feed people again. Land can be carefully plowed and preserved, and the soil itself can be carefully observed and given what it needs. That way crops grow up healthy and the tiny plants and animals in the soil stay healthy too.

Gardeners, farmers, and soil scientists are learning from each other and from farmers in other parts of the world how to take good care of the soil so it will continue to feed us and our children and our children's children. Maybe you can become one of the people who is doing this important work!

Soil Erosion Experiment

You need:

- two plates (aluminum pie plates are fine)
- mud pies
- a hose
- a three-minute timer

To make mud pies, mix up soil and water and put the pies into the pie plates. The pies should be about 1/2-inch thick. Let the pies dry thoroughly for a few days.

When the pies are dry, prop them up on some small stones so they are slightly tilted. Next, place the hose as shown in drawing 1, so water flows gently over the mud pie in a sheet. Let it flow for three minutes. What happens?

For the second plate, stand up and pretend you are a rainstorm. Let the water droplets from your hose hit the mud pie hard. What happens?

Your mud pies are unprotected soil. How is soil protected in a forest? In a meadow? How can we protect the soil in which we grow our food? (There is not just one answer to this question!)

Wormino's Wanderings

In this game, you are an earthworm. Your name is Wormino. You've had a great summer burrowing through a garden, but now it's time to go down deep where the cold can't reach. You have some word snacks along the way, but before you munch them, you have to match the word with the definition. When you finish, you'll have a letter and a number matched on your paper. Answers are printed at the bottom of the page.

Definitions

1. A kind of fungus that you can sometimes see growing on bread that's been left around too long. This is a hard worker in the process of decay.
2. Loss of soil.
3. A furry animal that is very good at making soil light and airy so plants can grow well.
4. Tiny animals that would look like eels if you could see them. They live among the roots of plants.
5. A kind of fungus you often see growing after lots of rain. All fungi use dead plants for food.
6. Material that has passed through an earthworm, often left at the entrance of a burrow. This material enriches the soil so plants can grow better.
7. Excellent soil makers who like to live under stones. They have hard bodies they curl up into balls when they are frightened.
8. The tiniest animals that live in soil. Amebas and flagellates are the two main kinds.
9. Rain, ice, and snow break rocks into tiny rocks to make soil.
10. Fungus and bacteria work to make plants and animals that have died into soil. The new soil then helps new plants and animals to grow.
11. Insects that haven't grown up yet. "Grubs" is another word for some of these creatures.
12. Going down, first there is plant material you can recognize, then tiny bits of plants too small to recognize, then more and more rock until finally there is solid rock.
13. Very helpful animals that break up soil and enrich it with their castings.

Answers

A. 9 H. 3
B. 5 I. 11
C. 10 J. 7
D. 1 K. 2
E. 13 L. 8
F. 6 M. 4
G. 12

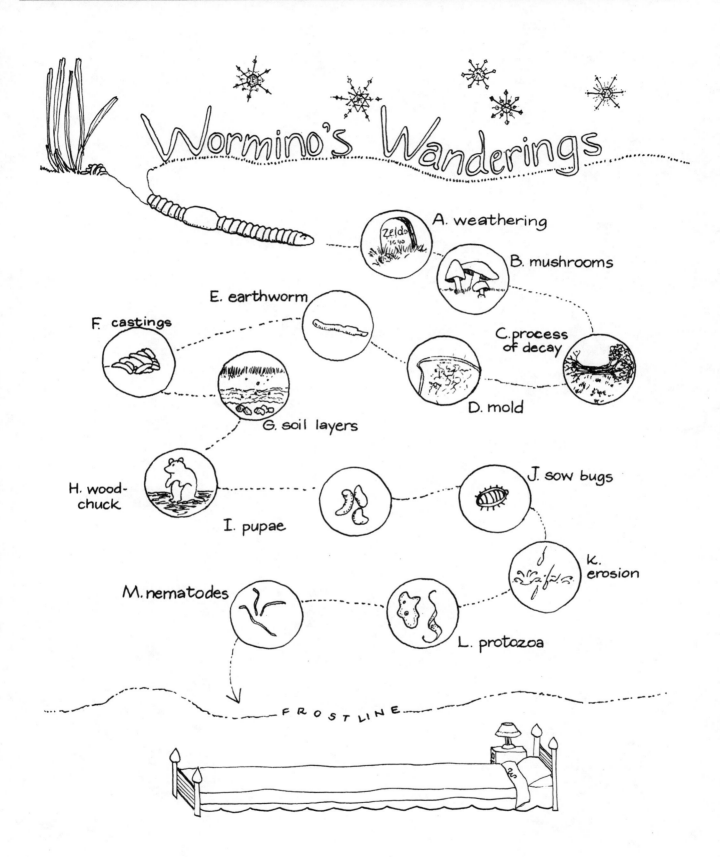

Wormino's Wanderings

A. weathering
B. mushrooms
C. process of decay
D. mold
E. earthworm
F. castings
G. soil layers
H. woodchuck
I. pupae
J. sow bugs
K. erosion
L. protozoa
M. nematodes

FROSTLINE

CHAPTER 4

Animals

How many animals have you seen in your life? Animals on television or in books don't count. How many different kinds of animals (and birds, fish, toads, and lizards) have you seen with your very own eyes?

List them on a sheet of paper.

How Many Animals?

Even though you had lots of space, you probably still ran out of room. Even if you live in the city and don't see many animals every day, you probably ran out of room on your paper. Sometimes you may have to think hard for a moment, but then you start remembering.

"There were those tropical fish in the pet store I watched for a long time. I don't remember their names, but there were lots of kinds there." Fish count.

"Oh, I forgot! Aunt Zelda has a pet ferret!" Ferrets count.

"I saw a mouse in the subway." Mice count, too.

People and Animals

People and animals go together.

Sometimes we may not like the animals who share the earth with us. Not many people like to share their houses with mice, for example. But even the animals we don't like have their own place in the world.

Mice, for example, are food for many animals. We may not like the fact that foxes, snakes, owls, and other animals eat mice. But mice are an important part of the food that many animals need to live. Foxes, for example, eat lots of berries. But they also need to eat "meat"—animals smaller than themselves, including mice.

Sometimes we just don't know about the animals who live near us. Maybe a weasel walked oh-so-softly under your basement window last night while she was hunting. Or maybe you never noticed the sparrow family nesting in the dry cleaner's sign at the end of the block.

And quite often we know about and love the animals who become a part of our lives. If you have a pet, you know how happy animals and people can be together. Or if you've watched a bird fly or a squirrel playing, and wished you could do that too, you know how nice animals can be.

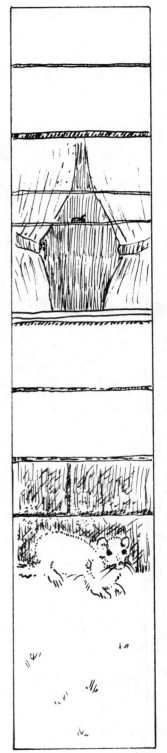

What Is an Animal?

You have probably spent some time in your life **classifying** things. Do you help with your family laundry by sorting socks? If you have only a few people in your family, and their feet are different sizes, that job is easy. If there are many people in your family and some of them are the same size, the job gets harder.

Scientists classify living things for the same reason you classify socks. You say, "These are grown-ups' socks and these are kids' socks," so you can put the socks into the right drawer.

Scientists say, "This creature is not a plant, it's an animal," so they know how to think about each living thing. Does it sound easy to divide living things into either plants or animals?

Actually, sometimes it's not. Until very recently, for example, scientists just didn't know whether to classify bacteria, those very tiny living things, as plants or as animals. For many years, one scientist would say they were plants, while another would say they were animals. There was a lot of confusion.

Finally, scientists agreed that bacteria were neither plants nor animals. They gave bacteria a separate category of their own.

Scientists divide living things into **kingdoms**. The two biggest kingdoms are plants and animals.

This chapter is about the animal kingdom, so all kinds of animals count. We often think of an animal as a creature with fur, four feet, and a tail, but fish, amphibians, and reptiles are animals too. So are birds, but because of their amazing ability to fly, they get a whole chapter to themselves in this book. And insects and spiders are animals, but they are so different that they get a chapter to themselves too.

What Do We All Need to Live?

Here is a list of what people need to live:

- air
- food
- water
- a way to stay warm
- a safe place to live and raise children

Can you think of anything to add to the list?
Here is a list of what animals need to live:

- air
- food
- water
- a way to stay warm
- a safe place to live and raise their young

Can you think of anything else an animal you know about would need to live?
Now look at the two lists. What do you notice when you compare them?

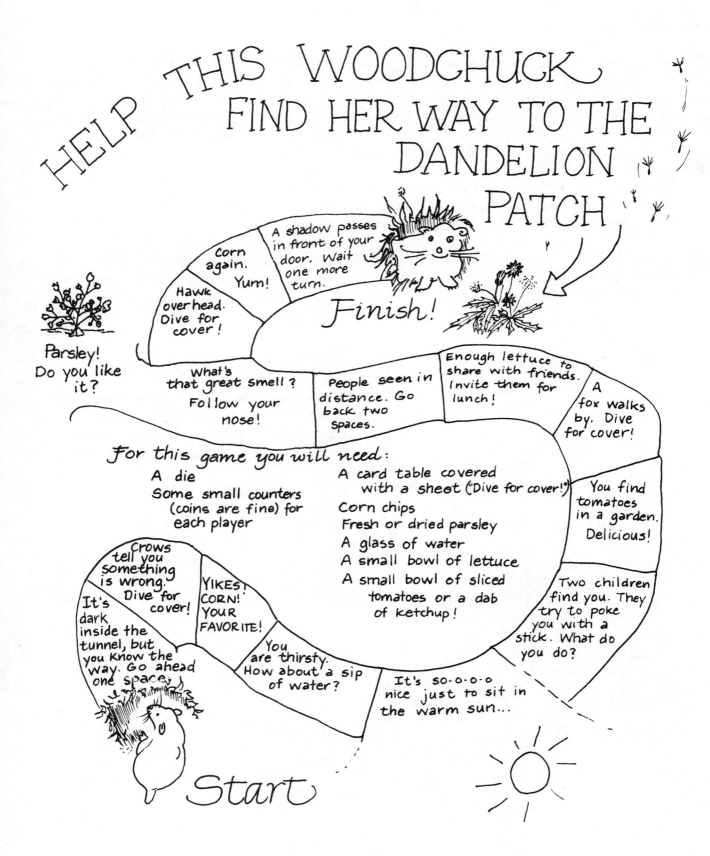

HELP THIS WOODCHUCK FIND HER WAY TO THE DANDELION PATCH

Finish!

Corn again. Yum!

A shadow passes in front of your door. Wait one more turn.

Hawk overhead. Dive for cover!

Parsley! Do you like it?

What's that great smell? Follow your nose!

People seen in distance. Go back two spaces.

Enough lettuce to share with friends. Invite them for lunch!

A fox walks by. Dive for cover!

For this game you will need:

A die
Some small counters (coins are fine) for each player

A card table covered with a sheet ("Dive for cover!")
Corn chips
Fresh or dried parsley
A glass of water
A small bowl of lettuce
A small bowl of sliced tomatoes or a dab of ketchup!

You find tomatoes in a garden. Delicious!

Two children find you. They try to poke you with a stick. What do you do?

Crows tell you something is wrong. Dive for cover!

It's dark inside the tunnel, but you know the way. Go ahead one space.

YIKES! CORN! YOUR FAVORITE!

You are thirsty. How about a sip of water?

It's so-o-o-o nice just to sit in the warm sun...

Start

69

Territories

We people have lots of different ways of getting what we need. We can go to a grocery store for food, or we can grow our own. We can go to a clothing store for clothes to keep us warm. A faucet gives us water to drink.

We have many different places to live. Some of us live in apartments, some of us live in condominiums, and some of us live in houses or mobile homes. Sometimes we can live in tents; or when we are camping in clear weather, all we need is a sleeping bag to sleep under the stars.

Think about where you get the things you need from day to day. Can you draw a picture of where you get your food, clothing, and the place where you live?

You have just drawn a picture of your **territory**.

Take a look at the picture on page 68. It is a drawing of a rabbit's territory. You can see where the rabbit finds food, water, and shelter. You can even see where a hawk sometimes perches, hoping to eat the rabbit for supper; but that rabbit is smart. Can you see in the drawing where the rabbit hides from the hawk?

Homes

Your home is important to you for many reasons. We often don't think a lot about some of the biggest reasons our homes are important. Where else can you go when it's too hot in the sun or when there is a late-night thunderstorm? Our homes are our shelter.

When we are children, our homes are safe places to grow up in.

When we are parents, our homes are safe places in which we raise our children.

Mystery Home

You can often predict what kind of a home an animal will live in if you know where it lives and what its habits are. Can you guess what kind of home this mystery animal lives in?

Mr. Marmota Monax loves to eat green leaves. Some of his favorites are clover, dandelion, chicory, and young vegetables in gardens. He can live in places at the edges of woods or in meadows.

In the winter he goes into a deep sleep until the spring.

When he wakes up from his hibernation, he will look for a Mrs. Marmota Monax, so they can start a family together. Then Mr. Monax leaves Mrs. Monax to raise the children alone.

The Monaxes are not very big. The little ones in the family can be food for hawks. Foxes, coyotes, and wolves may hunt the whole family.

Marmota Monax moves on four feet. Sometimes you can't even see his legs moving because his body is so close to the ground.

He has beautiful brown, glossy fur, small ears, and whiskers. He can't move very fast, but he doesn't have to. He is never very far away from one of the several entrances to his home.

Mystery Solved

Does Mr. Monax live in trees?

No.

He can live at the edges of woods, but he can also live in meadows. And he eats plants that grow on the ground, like dandelions.

How can he eat ground plants, not be able to move very fast, and still get to his home when he sees an enemy?

Mr. Marmota Monax and his family live in a burrow in the ground, that's how!

Marmota monax is the Latin name for woodchuck. Scientists use

the Latin names for plants and animals when they talk to each other to avoid confusion. A woodchuck in one part of the country may be called a groundhog in another part of the country.

If you guessed Mr. Monax is a marmot or a prairie dog, you would be right, too. Each of these animals has a complicated system of burrows with several entrances and exits, so they never need to run far when they are threatened. Not surprisingly, prairie dogs, marmots, and woodchucks are related to each other.

Where Do Animals Make Their Homes?

Furred or feathered animals can live in burrows in the ground, holes in trees, or in the holes left in the ground after a tree falls.

Can you find the chipmunk?

They can live in mounds they build in the middle of a pond, hills they make themselves, or inside thick, prickly piles of brush.

They can hollow out places in thick grass to call home. They can live in caves, or houses, or barns, or even abandoned cars. They can live in the middle of big cities or in places they know people won't be.

And of course some animals build nests. Birds aren't the only ones who do! Squirrels build nests, too. And black bears sometimes build temporary nests in trees.

Some kinds of fish can even build nests under water. A male stickleback fish will build a nest for a female who is ready to lay eggs. He builds it out of water plants and bits of roots and shapes it like a little tunnel on the sandy bottom of some shallow water.

Some animals carry their homes on their backs. Turtles do. Snails do, too. Sometimes, we laugh at the slow way these animals move, but maybe it would be handy, from their point of view, to always have a safe place to go.

Secret Animals

Maybe you know someone who goes hunting or is in the army who dresses in **camouflage** clothes, usually in green or brown. Camouflage clothes have a pattern of light and dark colors printed on them. These clothes help people look like they are part of the woods or fields. To an animal, they don't look like people at all.

Maybe you have some camouflage clothes yourself. Have you tried them out to see if they help you to become invisible in fields or woods?

People learned about camouflage from animals. Lots of animals grow their own "camouflage clothes."

Many kinds of birds have brown or gray streaked feathers that help them blend into the woods or fields where they live.

Frogs and toads are often so perfectly matched to their surroundings that we miss them as we walk by.

Snakes blend into leaf litter on a forest floor, grass in a field, or sandy desert soil so well that we often know they are there only if they begin to move.

Fish are sometimes patterned in a dark color on top, so fish-eating flying birds can't see them. These same fish may have light-colored bellies, so that enemies who look at them from below will think they are a part of the light-colored sky or surface of the water.

Have you ever noticed the stripes on a chipmunk's back? When you see a chipmunk out in the sun you might think he is easy to see. But when he is in the woods, where there are little spots of sun and shade on the ground, you can't easily see him if he is quiet.

When deer are first born, they have white spots on their fur, too. Here is what a baby deer, or fawn, will do most of the day the first few weeks after it is born:

It will lie *perfectly still*.

That is the best thing a fawn can do. That way, it will blend into the light-and-dark pattern on the floor of the woods where it is lying. An enemy can walk very close to a fawn and not know it is there!

Home Is Where the Run Is

Do you like to run? There is another meaning of the word "run" for animals. You can picture it by pretending you are a mouse.

Close to the hollow log where you live there is a drainage ditch where you go to drink whenever you are thirsty. How often during the day are you thirsty? You may be working on cleaning out your hole and you get thirsty, so down to the water you run. Or you hear a sound by the water, so down you run. Gathering seeds also makes you thirsty.

Soon your mouse's body will make a hollow tunnel in the grass that leads from your house to the water, because you go that way again and again. By running that way so often, you have made a mouse **run**.

Just as we make paths around our houses, gardens, and vacant lots with our feet, animals make them too. When a path is close to an animal's home and made by daily activities, we call it a "run." Runs can be tunnels, or matted grasses, or scraped-down-to-the-earth paths. Animals will use them over and over again.

With a little practice, you can become good at finding animal paths and runs. Look for places that are worn away. If you are lucky enough to live next to a field, look at the border of your yard. You'll probably see lots of places where animals come into your yard from the field.

In this drawing, you can see: a mouse run, a rabbit run, a fox hunting, a deer bed, and a woodchuck's entrance to his burrow.

74

Making Tracks

You have probably noticed how your feet leave prints in dusty, muddy, or snowy ground. Sometimes you can even tell what brand of sneaker people are wearing by the footprints, or **tracks**, they leave.

Have you ever looked at the bottom of a dog's or a cat's foot, then looked at the tracks they leave when they walk? If you know what the bottom of an animal's foot looks like, you can guess what its track will look like.

There are two ways to figure out which animal left a track you're interested in. You can go around catching animals and looking at the bottoms of their feet, but that might be a little difficult! Or, you can find a book about tracks or even a chart you can put up on your wall to help you learn who left tracks behind them as they walked.

Why would you want to do this? Well, tracks can tell you a story as clearly as any book can. Who came down to the stream last night? Who ran around in the dust by that new house that's being built, and who were they running from? And did they escape?

Who circled around your camp while you were asleep?

Sammy, a dog, leaves a track in the mud as he chases a squirrel.

Can you find them all?

75

Can you read this Track Story?

Some people are able to read tracks just like you are reading this book. They can tell not only what kind of animal the track belongs to, but often how old the track is, whether or not the animal was in a hurry, and even smaller details about the animal.

This track picture tells a simple story. Can you read the story? The key will help you, and so will the questions that go with the circled letters A through F on the map. Here's an extra hint: If you get stuck, read the story "Whose Life Is Luckier?" at the end of this chapter.

Questions

A 1. Where was the coyote standing when she saw the rabbit?

    2. Where did the rabbit go?

B 1. How did the coyote cross the stream?

C Lots has happened here.

    1. What do you think the people leaned up against the cliff?

(*Hint:* Backpackers always carry a _____.)

    2. While one person was building a fire, what did the two other people do?

    3. Where did all three people sit down to eat their supper?

    4. What did they see in their camp later that evening?

D 1. Why do the two people's tracks change when they get to the edge of the stream?

E 1. What does the coyote do to reach her den from the canyon floor?

F 1. Whose tracks go past the coyote's den?

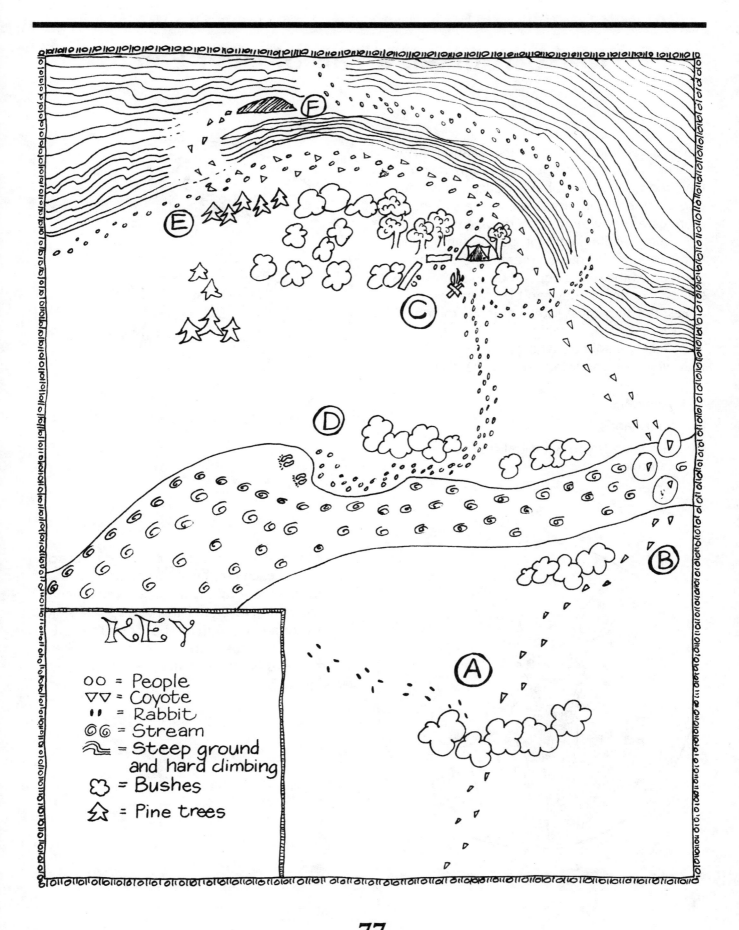

KEY

○○ = People
▽▽ = Coyote
'' = Rabbit
◎◎ = Stream
≈ = Steep ground and hard climbing
❀ = Bushes
☆ = Pine trees

Make Yourself a Pair of Deer Ears

Have you ever looked at an animal and noticed how its ears are different from yours? If you have a dog, you've probably noticed how your dog can move her ears to listen to a sound more carefully without even moving her head.

Many wild animals can do the same thing, but for them it's an even more important skill. Sometimes their lives depend upon standing as still as a stone, so they can't be seen by enemies. But they must listen carefully, to know what their enemy is doing.

Deer are animals who can move their ears that way. You can listen like a deer! You need:

- your ears,
- your hands,
- and sounds you want to listen to more carefully.

Make each hand into a cup, and put each cup behind each ear, bending the back of your ear toward the sound with each cupped hand. Can you hear a lot better this way?

Go to a place with a lot of sound to test your new deer ears. Can you tell exactly where some sounds are coming from, even with your eyes closed?

Animal Senses

You can learn a lot about animals from their tracks. You can also learn a lot about them simply by watching them.

If you have ever watched a rabbit closely, you know that when a rabbit hops across an open space where there isn't a place to hide, it is very cautious. The rabbit will hop a few steps, stop, and then twitch its ears all around.

How are rabbit ears different from yours?

For one thing, they are on the very top of a rabbit's head. They stick up into the air. Your ears are on the side of your head, and you can't move them very much. For another thing, those rabbit ears are BIG.

What are rabbits listening for?

As you know, rabbits are food for many other animals. Foxes, hawks, coyotes, wolves, lynxes, dogs, cats, and other animals all eat rabbits. Rabbits need those big ears to listen for enemies.

When you look at an animal, look at its ears. Where are the ears on its head and how big are they? Can the animal move them easily? The answers to these questions will give you a clue as to how well the animal can hear *you* if you want to sneak up close to watch it go about its business.

Animal Eyes

You've probably heard the expression "eagle eyes." All you have to do to understand that expression is imagine an eagle flying very high up in the sky while searching the ground far below for any movement that may mean a meal. A tiny mouse brushing against a plant stalk can be seen by an eagle so high up that to you the eagle might look like a small moving speck in the sky.

Do you think your own eyesight is that good? Probably not. But then, your life doesn't depend on how clearly you can see long distances to find your food.

Animals who hunt other animals for their food often have excellent eyesight. The animals they hunt may also have good eyesight so they can avoid their enemies.

How about bears? Their eyes look small compared to the rest of their bodies. We often think of bears as being fierce hunters.

But the truth is, bears seem to use their noses more than their eyes to find food. Often, their eyesight isn't very good. Many bears live mostly on plants and insects.

Most bears are shy of people. In national parks where hikers might meet bears, park rangers advise people to make lots of noise by clapping, talking loudly, or wearing jingle bells on their ankles. That way the shy bears have plenty of warning and disappear before people come down the path.

Fast Eyes

Some Native American scouts learned to use their eyes in different ways, depending on what they wanted to see. If they were concentrating on making a fish hook, for example, they used their eyes as we do, looking mostly at the work before them.

But when they went hunting, they could see a lot more than we usually do. They moved their eyes quickly from side to side without moving their heads much. They would not let their eyes rest on one thing, but instead looked all over. They could see any slight movement that way, or they could quickly spot anything that looked out of place, like a deer standing still in the middle of a grassy meadow.

Try this: Become aware of how your eyes tend to rest on the ground in front of you as you walk outdoors. Try moving your eyes around instead. (But first make sure you know where you will step next!)

Ask a friend to toss crumpled paper balls up in the air in the line with your outstretched arms. Can you see the balls when you look straight ahead? Pretend you're a young Native American brave in training.

"Fast eyes" will help you to see animals where you may not have seen them before. Do you think they may use their eyes the same way to see *you*?

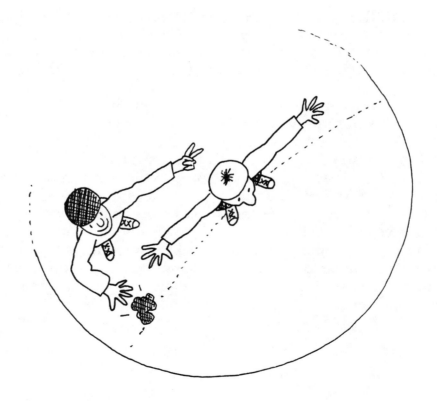

Animal Noses

How would you say your nose is different from a dog's nose? The color is different, and the shape of the nostrils is different. You know that dogs have a better sense of smell than people.

Part of the reason for a dog's, or a fox's, or a coyote's keen sense of smell is that their noses are at the end of their faces. It is easy for them to lift their noses into the wind to smell you coming, or to stick their noses into a woodchuck burrow to find out if anyone is home.

Animals who hunt other animals often have a keen sense of smell.

A fox lifts his nose into the wind.

Animals who are hunted by other animals also often have a keen sense of smell.

Here is a hint for you if you ever want to sneak up on an animal quietly: Before you start, wet your finger. The side of your finger that feels coldest and dries the fastest is the side the wind is blowing from.

You want to be down wind. You want the animal to be between you and the direction the wind is coming from, so the animal won't smell your smell floating by on the wind. The drawing shows you how to do this.

YOU are "down wind"

The wind is coming from that direction

Animal Tongues

Animals use their tongues while eating the same way we do. But some animals use their tongues in very different ways.

A lizard flicks her tongue.

Many lizards and all snakes flick their tongues in and out a lot. They are actually tasting the air. Both lizards and snakes have nostrils, but mostly they use their tongues to taste the air, rather than their noses to smell, where their prey might be.

We need all our senses, and it's hard to imagine other ways of learning about the world. Scientists know that snakes and many lizards "taste the air." They also know that some lizards and snakes can't hear as well as we can. But they can sense vibrations through the ground in a way that human beings cannot. They learn everything they need to know with their strange senses.

Some snakes, called pit vipers, are even able to sense tiny differences in temperature through little dents, or pits, on either side of their faces. Why would this be helpful to them? They can tell where frogs or mice are by their body warmth, even in total darkness. Frogs and mice are their main food.

Animals' Sense of Touch

Animals know when something brushes their skin, fur, or feathers, of course, just as you know when someone brushes against you in the hall.

Animals don't depend on their sense of touch to stay alive in the same way they depend on their other senses, though. A rabbit's ears or nose will tell the rabbit that a dog is coming long before the dog is close enough to be dangerous.

Some animals have whiskers. A mouse, for example, has long, sensitive whiskers that are very useful. Can you guess why?

Mice often live in dark nests and tunnels. They can't see the walls of their homes as they run through them, but their whiskers brush the walls in the dark before they can bump into them.

Fawn Magic

How can we get close enough to wild animals to really look at them?

The newborn fawn in the woods gives us the perfect answer.

Stay very still.

Try this: Pick a good place to see animals. Dress comfortably, in a color that will blend in with the background so that you are camouflaged. Find a place to sit. Pretend you are a stone and wait.

Here is a checklist to help you with your "fawn magic."

Your Place

1. Will animals find food and maybe water here?
2. Is there a good place for animals to hide if an enemy comes? (Ask yourself, "If I were four inches high, could I hide quickly here?")
3. Is it a good time of day to see animals? If you have seen animals in this place before, go there close to that time. Otherwise, early morning and evening are often good times.

Your Clothes

To sit still for a long time, you have to be comfortable.

1. Will you itch or tickle from grass or sit on twigs? Wear long pants.
2. Will you sit on damp ground? Bring a small plastic bag to sit on.
3. Are there lots of bugs? Wear long pants, long sleeves, and a hat. Try to avoid insect spray, since the smell may make some animals notice you.
4. Will the sun be hot? Wear long sleeves, light colors, and a hat. Again, avoid sun lotion because of the smell if you can.

You Yourself

1. Picture a stone in your mind.
2. Become that stone.
3. Does the stone talk?
4. Does the stone scratch its ear?
5. Does the stone slap at flies?
6. Does the stone see animals eating, playing, and teaching their little ones because animals don't even notice it is there?

P.S. Stones are allowed to sneeze if they have to!

Where's Home?

If you want to find out where an animal lives, sometimes you can follow its tracks or runs to find its nest or burrow. Sometimes you can find an animal's home by accident when you explore woods or fields. Sometimes you know very well where an animal lives if it lives in or near your home!

Just like us, animals need to stay warm, dry, and safe.

Kinds of Animals

What's a Mammal?

We often think of an animal as a creature with four feet, fur, and a tail. Squirrels, opossums, rabbits, deer, and bears have four feet, fur, and a tail. So do dogs, cats, and many other kinds of animals. All these animals are **mammals**.

Mammals need to keep their insides at exactly the right warm temperature all the time, no matter what the temperature of the air or water is that surrounds the outside of their bodies. They do it automatically. Mammals are **warm-blooded**.

Mammal mothers also feed their babies with milk from their own bodies.

So mammals may be furry, and may have four feet and a tail (in fact, most mammals do), but there are two things all mammals have: warm blood and the ability to feed their young with mother's milk.

Amphibians Have Two Lives

There are many other kinds of animals besides mammals. You could probably name some right now. What about frogs, toads, and salamanders? They are **amphibians**. "Amphibian" means "an animal with two lives."

What does having "two lives" mean? The group of animals we call amphibians has those "two lives" because their "childhoods" are so different from their "adulthoods." Take a toad, for instance. Who would ever guess that the delicate-looking tadpole swimming in the pond would turn into the toad with four legs and very bumpy skin who hunts for bugs in a garden?

An amphibian's first life is spent in or very near the water. Young amphibians breathe in water. When they grow up, they need air to breathe, but they will still stay in or near the water. You would, too, if you got all the water you needed through your skin!

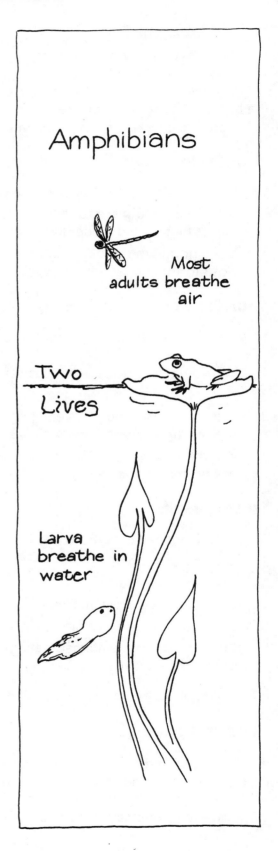

Amphibians

Most adults breathe air

Two Lives

Larva breathe in water

Amphibians are also **cold-blooded**. That means that instead of keeping their blood at the same warm temperature, as mammals do, they can live with their blood closer to the temperature of the air or water that surrounds them. To be active, though, amphibians need to keep fairly warm. That is why you may see a frog sitting in the morning sun. He is getting himself warm after the cool night, so he can be up and start his day's business of hunting for insects to eat.

Frogs and Toads

You know that frogs live in or very near the water, and that toads prefer moist, but not always watery, places. You might know that both frogs and toads begin as eggs and hatch into tadpoles before they become adults. And frogs and toads certainly look very much alike. How can you tell the difference?

The easiest way to tell the difference between frogs and toads is to look at their skin. Toads' skins are very bumpy. Some people call these bumps "warts," and they say you can get warts by touching toads. You can understand why people came to believe this when you learn that some toads' bumps make a liquid that tastes very nasty to any animal that tries to eat a toad for dinner. People can get the liquid on their hands if they handle a toad roughly. The liquid doesn't cause warts. Do wash your hands after handling toads, though. Some people can get a rash after handling a toad.

There are other differences between frogs and toads. Both frogs and toads lay their eggs in water, but frogs lay their eggs so they look like jelly clouds. Toads lay their eggs so they look like jelly strings.

Toads spend the winter hidden in the ground. Frogs mostly escape the cold by burrowing into mud. Toads often eat at night, and frogs more often eat by day.

And frogs generally prefer to avoid people. They will hop away quickly if you come too close. Toads, if you come to them quietly, will often let you watch them. Sometimes you can even get close enough to scratch a toad's back! Toads seem to enjoy that very much.

The difference between a toad and a frog

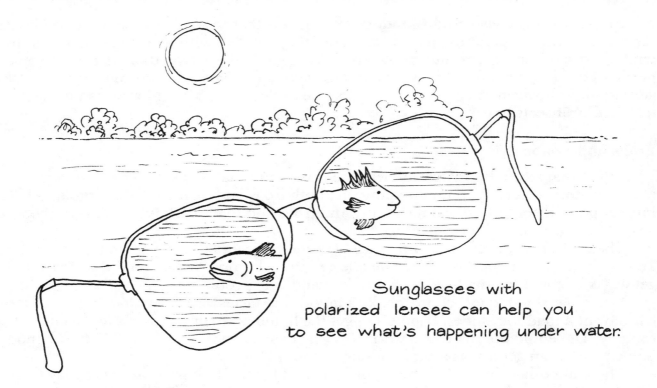

Sunglasses with
polarized lenses can help you
to see what's happening under water.

Salamanders

Salamanders are also amphibians. Many kinds of salamanders actually live in the water most of their lives. Other kinds of salamanders need places that are moist, but not watery. Look for salamanders under stones and rotting logs. Be very gentle, though. Salamanders are very shy.

Fish Are Animals, Too

Have you ever thought about how perfectly shaped fish are for moving through the water? Water flows smoothly over their bodies as they swim. Even the surfaces of their skins help the water to slip around them as they move, because their scales are fitted so tightly together. Their bodies are

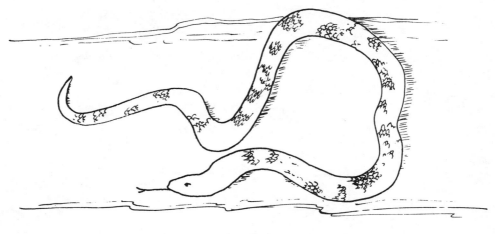

A snake basking in the sun

coated with a slime that helps them move smoothly and prevents diseases, too.

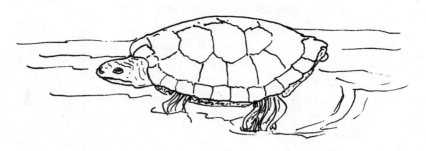

It's often difficult to see fish, even though you know there may be quite a few of them in a pond or stream. Fish are often so well camouflaged that they are "invisible."

Sometimes, especially on a sunny day, it is almost impossible to see below the surface of the water because of the sun's glare. Try wearing a pair of polarized sunglasses to look below the surface of the water. (Just put them on. You don't even have to put your face close to the water. Try standing in different places to see which place works best.) You may see a mysterious fish shape slowly moving among the weeds that you couldn't see before.

Reptiles

What is absolutely the largest reptile you can think of?

Hint: It doesn't have to be living on the earth right now.

If you named one of the largest dinosaurs, like the apatosaurus in the picture at the beginning of this book, you would be right. Dinosaurs were **reptiles**. That means that turtles, lizards, alligators, and snakes are relatives of the dinosaurs. Maybe some dinosaur relatives even live in your own back yard!

All reptiles have scales. Scales grow from a reptile's skin and help the animal to protect itself from other animals. Scales are very hard.

All reptiles are cold-blooded. Like amphibians, they must find ways to warm up when they are becoming too cool, or to cool off if they are becoming too warm. Have you ever seen a snake basking in the sun early on a summer morning? If the snake moves more slowly than you might expect, that is because it still isn't entirely warmed up from a cool night. What would it be like if you had to find a sun spot and sit a while before you could move freely in the morning?

Turtles

Turtles are reptiles who have been around a long, long time. There were turtles before dinosaurs. There were turtles while dinosaurs were the biggest animals on earth. Turtles were there as the dinosaurs disappeared. Turtles are living in ponds and in deserts (tortoises are turtles who live in dry places) today.

Turtles are tough animals. Maybe they have been around so long because of their hard shells. They move slowly because of the weight and awkward shape of those shells. But maybe the fact that they can tuck most of their bodies into their shells when danger comes near makes up for their slowness.

Lizards

Some people confuse salamanders and lizards. If you don't look too closely, their long thin bodies, long tails, and four legs do make the two different kinds of animals look alike. But salamanders have smooth moist skin. (Their skin has to be moist because that's how they get their water.) Salamanders also have fewer than five toes. Lizards have scaly skin and five toes with claws.

If lizards think about it, they must especially appreciate their tails. Their tails help them to keep their balance as they scamper along deck rails and tree limbs. Their tails are often very colorful and long. Their tails can help them when they must go for a long time without food: They can store fat in their tails, which they can use when they need it to stay alive.

Many kinds of lizards have a special secret weapon in their tails. No, they don't shoot poison darts or anything like that. But when an enemy gets too close to some kinds of lizards, all the enemy ends up with is a wriggling, sometimes very colorful, lively looking *tail*! The rest of the lizard has escaped!

Snakes

Snakes are reptiles who don't have eyelids or ears. And they don't have legs or feet, either. So how can they move?

Can you figure out how they move by watching them?

Scientists have figured out how snakes move by using slow motion photography.

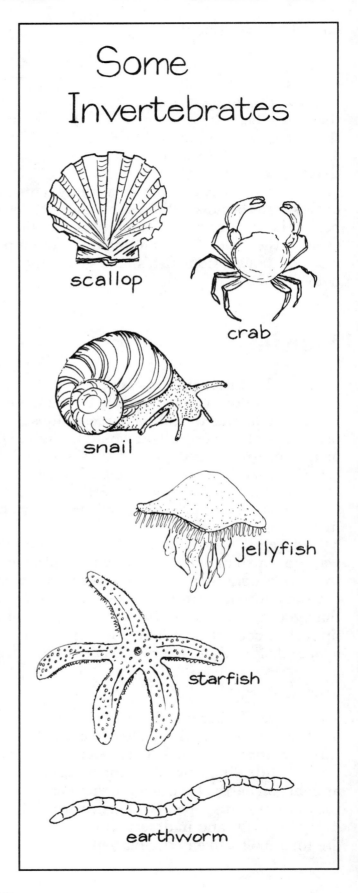

Some Invertebrates

scallop

crab

snail

jellyfish

starfish

earthworm

They found out that snakes can use two different ways to get around. The first way won't surprise you if you have ever watched a snake move. Snakes can "push off" from several places on their bodies at the same time.

The second way some snakes move is by flexing their skeletons and muscles in a complicated way. The snakes' skins and bodies are pulled along too.

No Backbone

Mammals, fish, amphibians, and reptiles, although they are very different in many ways, all have backbones. Scientists call all animals who have backbones **vertebrates**. Backbones help an animal to move and give an animal's body its shape.

Are there any animals without backbones?

There are plenty of animals who live very happily without backbones! They are called **invertebrates**. You can usually tell just by looking at an animal whether or not it has a backbone that helps it to keep its shape.

Slugs are a perfect example. Snails, their close relatives, are another. A backbone would just get in the way of a slug's or a snail's smooth, gliding way of moving. Both kinds of animals move along slowly on "sidewalks" that they make themselves. Have you ever seen a silvery line leading over a stone, with a slug or a snail at the end of it? These two kinds of animals glide along a path of slime that they make themselves from a place at the front part of their one "foot."

How does a snail move?

The next time you find a garden snail, put the snail into a clear glass and watch as it moves up the side of the glass. You can see up close how the snail moves up on its one "foot."

If you live near or have visited the ocean, you know about many animals without backbones. Jellyfish float in the water, trailing tentacles that sting the small animals they eat. (Jellyfish can also sting people, so it's best to stay away from them, even if they are washed up on a beach.)

Scallops, clams, oysters, barnacles, and all other kinds of shellfish are invertebrates. Sponges are, too.

On land, there is a kind of very common invertebrate who lives in the soil. Quite a few of them may be eating their way through the soil nearest you at this very moment. Who are they?

Earthworms! Earthworms don't have backbones, but they seem to do very well without them. Since earthworms are very important to healthy soil, you can find out more about them in Chapter 3, about soil.

Insects are also invertebrates. They don't have backbones, but as adults, they can have very rigid shapes because of their exoskeletons. You can read about insects in their own chapter, Chapter 6.

People Are Animals, Too

The animal kingdom includes many different kinds of animals, doesn't it? Toads, fish, earthworms, centipedes, and spiders are all animals. So are the warm-blooded animals—including birds, raccoons, cougars, mice, and many others.

We are mammals, too. So some people say we are animals and leave it at that. Other people say that to call us "animals" is true, but it isn't the whole truth. They say that we are able to love each other and to learn about and love the natural world in a way no

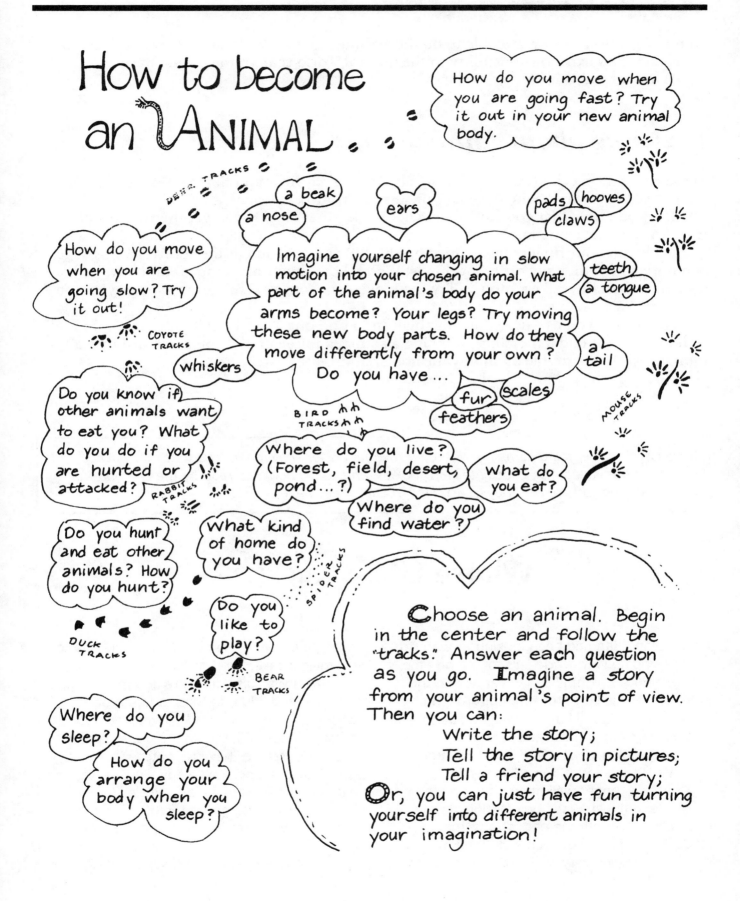

How to become an ANIMAL

How do you move when you are going fast? Try it out in your new animal body.

DEER TRACKS

How do you move when you are going slow? Try it out!

COYOTE TRACKS

Do you know if other animals want to eat you? What do you do if you are hunted or attacked?

RABBIT TRACKS

Do you hunt and eat other animals? How do you hunt?

DUCK TRACKS

What kind of home do you have?

Do you like to play?

BEAR TRACKS

Where do you sleep?

How do you arrange your body when you sleep?

a beak
a nose
ears
pads hooves
claws
teeth
a tongue

Imagine yourself changing in slow motion into your chosen animal. What part of the animal's body do your arms become? Your legs? Try moving these new body parts. How do they move differently from your own? Do you have...

whiskers
a tail
fur scales
feathers

BIRD TRACKS

Where do you live? (Forest, field, desert, pond...?)

What do you eat?

Where do you find water?

SPIDER TRACKS

MOUSE TRACKS

Choose an animal. Begin in the center and follow the "tracks." Answer each question as you go. Imagine a story from your animal's point of view. Then you can:
Write the story;
Tell the story in pictures;
Tell a friend your story;
Or, you can just have fun turning yourself into different animals in your imagination!

animal can. Because we are able to do these things that animals can't, they say, human beings have an extra responsibility to the natural world that animals can't have.

What do you think?

Learning about Animals

There isn't any special trick to learning about animals' lives and homes. Books can help a lot, but your eyes and ears, nose and fingers are your best teachers.

Did you know that you can smell where a deer has slept if you get there soon enough? It's a kind of barnyard smell.

Feel with your fingers how a bird has built its nest. Listen to the squirrels' language, and notice how they say different things. Watch how slowly a cat moves and how he holds his head when he stalks a mouse. Try the movements out yourself, even though you don't have four legs.

Best of all, you can use your imagination to find out what an animal's life might really be like. If you spend a morning watching a squirrel, for example, you can "turn into a squirrel" with no trouble at all in your imagination.

Two children are going camping with their favorite uncle. They made sure that they packed plenty of hot cocoa mix, chocolate chip cookies, and comic books to read by the campfire for their camping trip. Before they go to sleep at camp they have a visitor. . . .

Whose Life Is Luckier?

Eduardo and Rita had been looking forward to going camping with Uncle Luis for a long time. Finally, a Friday night in spring came, and the twins and Uncle Luis drove to a dirt road in the mountains. "We will have to walk a little to get to our first camp," Uncle Luis said.

"We walk a lot at home," said Eduardo.

"We RUN a lot at home," Rita said.

It was a longer walk than they thought it would be, but just as the twins' shoulders began to ache from the pack straps, they stopped at a place between a cliff and a stream. It smelled very nice. There were some small pine trees close by. Eduardo and Rita took off their sneakers and socks and waded in the stream. Uncle Luis built a fire and made supper.

Rita and Eduardo tried to figure out if it was one fish or two that kept making ripples in a still pool. Uncle Luis told them they couldn't get any closer, so they just watched.

Finally, supper was ready. Supper was beans and corn tortillas, and Uncle Luis had fried some eggs to go on top of the beans.

The twins were hungry, and the food was good.

While they were eating supper, it got dark.

Suddenly, Eduardo gasped. "What's that?" he asked Uncle Luis. He saw a fast-moving, light-brown shadow at the edge of the camp.

"A coyote," said Uncle Luis.

"I bet that coyote's cold and that's why he came to find our fire," said Rita. Then she laughed. "Poor coyote! No chocolate chip cookies!" she said, taking a big bite out of hers.

"Poor coyote! No hot chocolate!" said Eduardo.

"Poor coyote! No tortillas!" said Rita.

"Poor coyote! No blankets to sleep in!"

"Poor coyote! No comic books to read in bed!"

"Poor coyote! No flashlight!"

"Poor coyote! No jacket when it gets cold!"

It was getting cold, and it was time to go to bed anyway. "I don't think we'll sleep under the sky after all," Uncle Luis said, looking at the sky. "Can you help me pitch the tent?"

Rita and Eduardo helped put up the tent, and soon everyone was sound asleep.

In the middle of the night they were awakened by a flash of lightening. Soon the thunder came, and lots of rain.

Their tent collapsed! Eduardo and Rita helped Uncle Luis pack up the tent quickly. By the time they packed up camp and pulled on their packs, they were wet to their skins.

And Uncle Luis made them take the high trail back to the car because he was afraid of being caught in a flood.

93

It was a long way back to the car. It was hard for Eduardo and Rita to climb up the steep trail, even with their flashlights. They were cold, and wet, and their wet pack straps rubbed into their shoulders.

They passed close to the coyote mother asleep in her den under a big rock. She was warm and dry, and so were her pups. They all slept together with their bushy tails curled up under their noses. She opened one eye as the backpackers passed by, but fell back asleep because she knew they couldn't see her.

Who was luckier that night?

Don't let Eduardo, Rita, and Uncle Luis's experience keep you from having a wonderful time when you camp. What can you do to have a good time?

■ *Bring the right clothes for the weather. Don't forget that the weather can change, even in the summer. A slightly chilly rain with a little wind can feel very cold if you have no slicker or warm clothes.*

■ *Choose your campsite carefully. Don't camp in a place where there might be flash floods.*

■ *Bring along a favorite toy or two, just in case you get bored. But see how many things you can see that grownups don't notice! Ask lots of questions!*

CHAPTER 5

Birds

Have you ever wondered what your home would look like from away up in the air?

Think about the building where you live. You know what it looks like when you walk toward it. You know what it looks like when you are riding in a car or bus.

What would your home look like if you could fly toward it and perch on a windowsill?

As a person with two legs, but no wings, you have to pay attention to where you walk. "Watch out for the street! Don't fall in that hole! Don't step in that mud!"

Most birds can walk. Most birds can also fly. You have to pay attention to the ground in front of you when you walk. Birds have to watch in front of them when they fly, too, but they also have to be careful about their "up and down" directions.

Do you sometimes wonder how they do it? Birds can fly through trees and not brush against a single twig. They fly under power lines and around houses, over small trees and under bigger ones. They are often in the air, but they never hit each other. And sometimes they seem to fly just for the fun of it! Have you ever watched a crow playing with the wind?

You can name some creatures who can fly who aren't birds. Insects and bats have wings, but no feathers. There are even some flying fish that can lift themselves up off the surface of the water, but they certainly don't have feathers.

Only birds have feathers.

Feathers

Feathers Are Like Baskets

Have you ever held a basket up to the light? Even though a basket can hold lots of things, it's full of holes!

A feather has holes too. The holes are so small that you can't see them. But a feather, even with the holes, can catch the air as easily as a bread basket holds bread. Bread doesn't fall through the holes in the basket, and air can't go through the holes in a feather.

If you do the "mystery drawing," you will weave those tiny lines in Step 4 together just like a basket. The white spaces are the holes.

Mystery Drawing

Here is a drawing you can copy on your own paper.

Step 1.

Draw this shape.

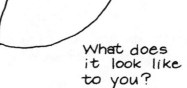

What does it look like to you?

Step 2.

Draw two lines in the middle, from the top to a little past the bottom.

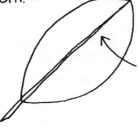

Right here the two lines begin to join.

Step 3.

Draw seven "V" shapes. The first two are drawn already.

Step 4.

Now draw lots of little "V"s coming off the ones you just drew, just as in the drawing here.

Don't worry if the "V"s overlap and look messy. They are supposed to be that way! Make the lines "weave" together. Fill in the two center lines.

Step 5.

Look at your drawing.

What does it look like?

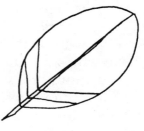

Does it look like a feather?

Why Does a Feather Have Holes?

A bird has to be very light to be able to fly. One reason we can't fly (besides the fact that we don't have wings) is because we weigh a lot. Birds weigh less than we do, not only because they are smaller, but also because:

1. Their bones are strong, but have air spaces inside them to make them weigh less; and
2. Their feathers are woven tightly together, but still have tiny air spaces to make them weigh less. Feathers make a bird "as light as a feather"!

Flying

Have you ever watched a duck take off from the water? His wings, and feathers, are spread very wide, to catch as much air as possible.

Have you ever watched a tree swallow or a barn swallow fly? Her wings are pointed and close to her body, so she's very fast and is catching as little air as possible.

All birds have wings that are shaped so that air will flow more quickly over the top of the wing than it flows over the bottom of the wing. The shape of a bird's wing turns it into an **air foil**. The wings of an airplane are shaped like an air foil, just like a bird's wings. You can make an air foil yourself if you follow the directions in the experiment "Flying paper, flying wings."

A tree swallow's wings are pointed for flying fast.

A duck takes off from the water with powerful wingstrokes.

Wing Feathers

Wing feathers have to be very strong because they have air rushing over and under them when the bird is flying. Wing feathers are different shapes and sizes, depending on where they are on the wing and what kind of flying the bird does.

The strongest wing feathers of all are the big ones that a bird stretches out while flying. They are the **primary flight** feathers. A primary flight feather has a short side that cuts into the wind, and a longer side that helps the air flow over the wing. The drawing of a bird's wing will help you to see how a primary feather works.

Flying paper, flying wings

An experiment

You need: a piece of notebook paper and scissors

1. Make a long, thin strip of paper from your notebook paper: Fold your paper in half lengthwise,

then lengthwise again,

and cut a strip from the side without holes.

2. What do you think will happen if you blow on top of the paper? Hold one end against your chin and see.

3. You have made an air foil!

How it works:

On which side of the paper is the air moving faster, the bottom or the top?

You make the air go faster over the top of the paper when you blow on it. Fast-moving air presses down less on the top of the paper, so the air that isn't moving underneath presses upward. Up goes the paper!

A bird's (and an airplane's) wing works the same way:

The shape of a bird's wing forces air to move more quickly over the top of the wing than it does underneath.

99

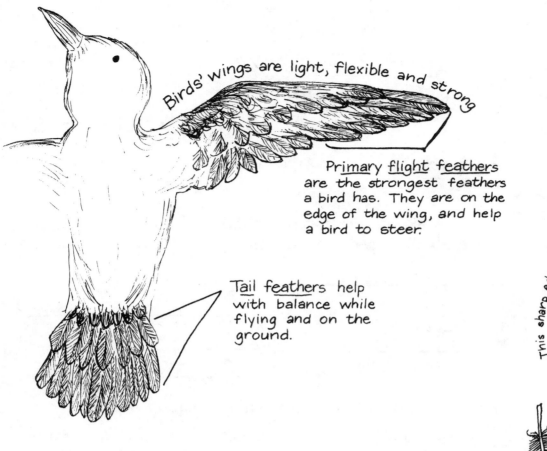

Birds' wings are light, flexible and strong

Primary <u>flight</u> <u>feathers</u> are the strongest feathers a bird has. They are on the edge of the wing, and help a bird to steer.

T<u>ai</u>l f<u>eath</u>ers help with balance while flying and on the ground.

This sharp edge cuts into wind

Flight feather

Tail feather

Body feather

Down feather

Tail Feathers

The kind of feather you drew in the "mystery drawing" is a tail feather. It is from the middle of a bird's tail. Tail feathers that grow from either side of the center of the tail may be slightly thicker on the side that is closest to the center of the tail. The drawing will help you to understand how feathers grow on most birds' tails.

Birds use tail feathers for steering through the air and to keep their balance on the ground or on a perch.

Some birds have very fancy tail feathers, especially male birds. Have you ever seen a male peacock displaying his big, bright feathers to a female?

Other Feathers

Body feathers streamline a bird's body for flying. Body feathers fit over each other like tile on a roof or like the scales on a fish. They are like a smooth coat for the bird.

Underneath the body feathers, birds have **down** feathers. All birds have lots of these. They're soft and fluffy, and they also catch lots of air and hold the air close to a bird's body, where the bird's body warmth heats it and helps to keep the bird warm.

Have you ever seen a bird sitting still on a cold day? That bird is probably all fluffed up to stay warm. Those are down feathers you see keeping the bird warm from tail to chin.

Some birds even use their own down feathers to line their nests to keep their baby birds warm.

And people use down feathers from ducks, geese, or chickens to stuff pillows, comforters, and jackets. We can be as warm as baby birds!

Finding Feathers

Birds' feathers can get raggedy and less and less useful as time goes on. Birds use their feathers when they are finding food, building nests, and feeding their little ones. Even the constant careful preening birds do just isn't enough to keep the feathers good enough for flying. Their feathers wear out just like your clothes do. So once a year, or sometimes more for some kinds of birds, a bird will shed its feathers. The process is called **molting**.

You can often find these feathers lying on the ground in the spring and early summer, and again in the late summer and fall.

Owls are almost silent as they fly. Not even the movement of their wings makes much of a sound.

Pigeon's flight feather

Owl's flight feather

They can catch a mouse almost without being heard. Do you think the edges of their flight feathers have anything to do with their silence?

101

But be careful. When you find a feather outdoors, be sure to wash your hands after handling it. Sometimes fresh bird feathers have tiny bugs called "mites" that lived on the bird and might want to live on you, too, even though you don't have feathers!

How Does a Feather Work?

A feather feels so light in your hand. If you hold it up to the sun, the sun shines through it. But you know that no air goes through it when you wave it through the air. A feather is strong. It has to be, to help a bird fly.

Take a look at the drawing "Figuring Out Feathers." The drawing will show you different things you can do with a feather that will help you to learn how a feather is put together.

At the center of the feather is the **shaft**. It is hollow. Why do you think it is hollow rather than solid?

Growing out from either side of the shaft are the **barbs**. You can see the barbs easily. The barbs don't look smooth, though. They look "sticky." They are almost like miniature feathers themselves, because from the barbs grow the **barbules**, tiny hairlike structures that stick together. Barbules grow from barbs just as barbs grow from the central shaft.

You can see the barbules growing from the barbs if you look very carefully. What you can't see, because they are too tiny, are the little hooks at the ends of the barbules.

Fluffy birds

You can paint this bird who has fluffed up all her feathers to stay warm on a cold winter morning.

1. Wet your paper with plain water. Take your brush, load it with paint, and touch it gently, just once, to the paper. What happens?

2. Now you wait till the paper dries. It will take a long time. Do something else for a while! Or you can use a hair dryer (with an adult's help) to speed it along.

These tiny hooks are very important, even though you can't see them. The hooks at the end of one barbule attach to the hooks at the end of the barbule across from it. The hooks weave together to make a "basket" that catches the air. The drawing on page 105 may help you to understand how all the little parts of a feather fit together so neatly.

You can prove to yourself that the tiny hooks are there. Have you ever "unzipped" a feather? The tiny hooks fit together much like the teeth of a zipper. You can pull them apart and put them back together again like you do a zipper on a jacket. The feather wouldn't unzip if the hooks weren't there.

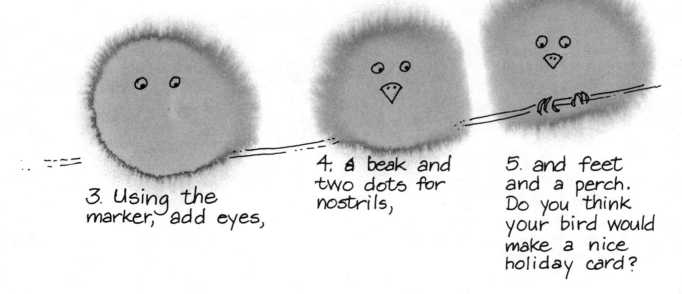

You need: watercolor paper, watercolor paint, a brush, a marker, and either lots of patience or a hair dryer and an adult.

3. Using the marker, add eyes,

4. a beak and two dots for nostrils,

5. and feet and a perch. Do you think your bird would make a nice holiday card?

Take a large shallow box, like a gift box for a sweater, and pin the feathers to the bottom of the box. Then you can cover the box with plastic wrap stretched tight and taped. Hang your box on the wall.

Put feathers between the pages of a book. But you'd better know which book on the shelf they are in, or you'll get a fluffy surprise one day!

BIG BOOK

You can put them in envelopes, and keep the envelopes in a box. Arrange the envelopes so you can flip through them the same way you flip through a library's card catalogue.

Before putting the feathers into your collection, put them into a plastic bag. Put the bag into a freezer for two weeks. No more lice or mites!

Start a feather collection
with molted feathers birds leave behind

You can arrange the feathers on a sheet of paper and put some clear sticky plastic over them VERY CAREFULLY. It helps to hold your breath! You'll want to do this only if you know you won't want to handle them again.

Take a piece of clear tape and tape each feather carefully to a piece of drawing paper. Draw a picture of where you found it, and date the picture.

Take all your feathers and poke them into a straw hat. That way you can wear your feather collection!

REMEMBER: Always wash your hands after handling fresh feathers.

Figuring Out Feathers

Take a closer look at a feather. To do this, you will need:

- a feather (of course!)
- a hand lens ("magnifying glass")
- a few drops of water
- an old toothbrush

Step 1. Do you know how to use a hand lens?

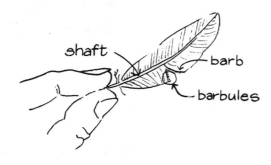

You can use it to see the tiny parts of a feather better by moving it up and down between your eyes and the feather until the feather is very clear. What do you see? Here are the parts of the feather you can see.

Step 2. Look at the pointed part of the shaft, the part that was attached to the bird. Is it solid or hollow? Would it help the bird to be heavier or lighter in the air?

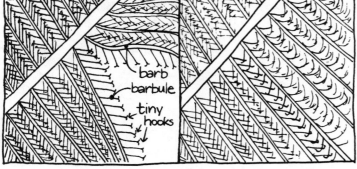

Step 3. Now take the feather and pull some of the barbs on one side apart. They seem to stick together, don't they? And if you listen very carefully, you can hear them "unzip," just like a zipper on a jacket.

If you had a microscope, which helps you to see things even smaller, you could see what look like tiny hooks growing off of the barbules. They fit together just like the teeth of a zipper do. They are what you heard "unzip" when you pulled the barbs and barbules apart.

Step 4. Gently tear apart lots of barbs and barbules. Now take the feather firmly between your fingers and flutter it through the air. Would you trust this feather to help you fly if you were a bird?

Step 5. Put a few drops of water on your feather. Does the feather soak up the water, does the water go through the tiny holes, or does the feather resist the water?

Step 6. Now take your toothbrush or use your fingers and smooth the feather gently, starting on the shaft at each side and moving out. You've "preened" the feather, just like a bird does! Even though the hooks are too small to see, you can see in the drawing what happened to them when you "preened" the feather.

Flutter the feather through the air now. Does it feel any different?

Look at the feather under the hand lens. It looks perfect, doesn't it?

Birds spend lots of time each day preening their feathers so they can fly. They depend on those feathers, so they have to be perfect.

Preening Birds

Confused? If you were a bird, you wouldn't be confused at all. Whenever your hooks became unhooked (and they become unhooked frequently), all you would do is run your beak up against the feather to hook them up again.

Have you ever watched birds preening? They are hooking together their tiny hooks! Birds are fixing their feathers when they preen so there aren't big holes in them that would let the air through when they fly. The drawing on page 105 shows you how a part of a feather might look before and after a bird preens it.

Birds also use oil when they are preening. They fetch the oil from preening glands that are near their tails. The oil makes their feathers water-resistant, so that water never reaches a bird's skin to chill the bird.

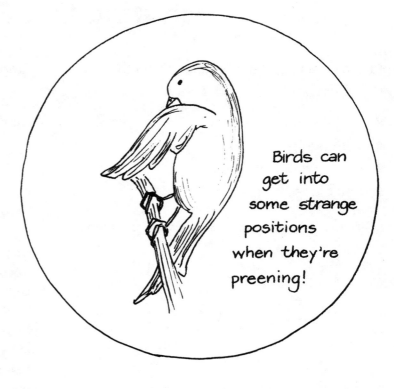

Birds can get into some strange positions when they're preening!

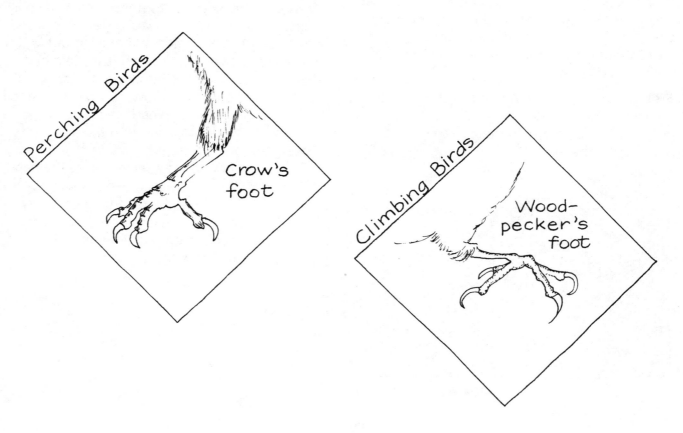

Perching Birds

Crow's foot

Climbing Birds

Wood-pecker's foot

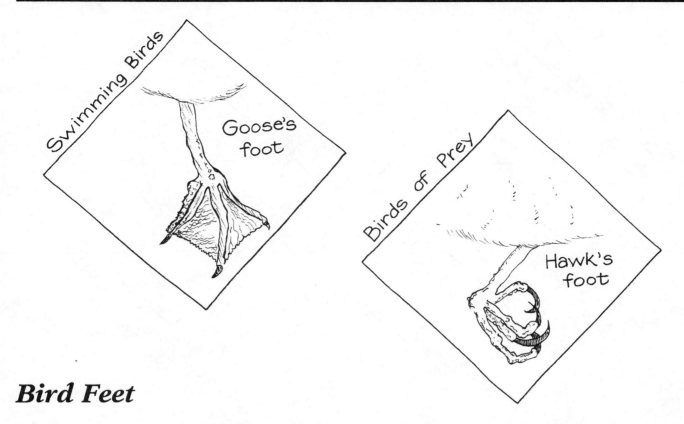

Bird Feet

Birds have wings where we have arms. We can't fly, but they can't hug another bird or pick up things with their wings, either.

Birds' feet are very different from our own. Each different kind of bird has feet that are perfect for the way that particular bird lives.

Perching birds have a hind toe for grasping their perches. The drawing of the crow's foot shows the big hind toe and the front toes with their hooked claws. Perching birds can hang onto their perches even in strong winds if they have to.

Some kinds of birds need to grasp tightly onto tree trucks. Woodpeckers eat insects that live inside tree bark. Woodpeckers have two hind toes and two front toes and strong toenails for clinging onto a tree.

Birds that swim in water have webbed feet. If you have ever gone swimming with flippers on your feet, you know how useful webbed feet can be to a duck!

Birds that hunt other animals have to have feet that can hold their prey firmly. The sharp **talons**, or claws, on a hawk, eagle, or owl help the bird to kill its prey quickly and to carry it away to a safe place to eat.

Beaks

You have probably noticed how very different birds' beaks are from one another. Why does the parrot in the pet store have a hooked beak and why do the sparrows on the side of the road have short pointy beaks?

The parrot's beak is made for tearing into fruit, its natural food. Parrots also have strong jaws for breaking apart seeds.

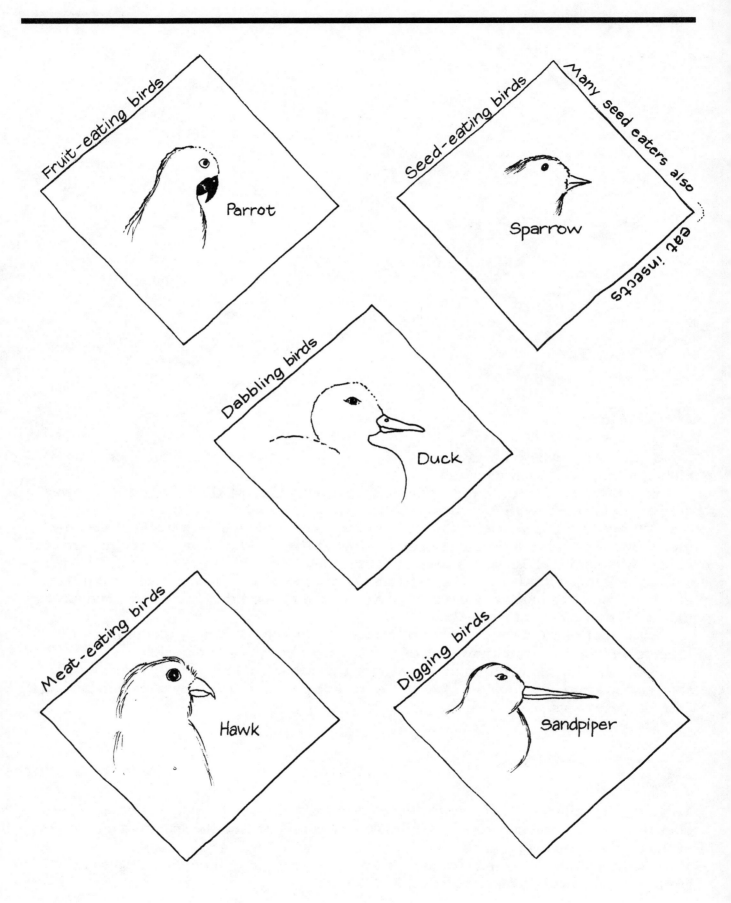

Fruit-eating birds

Parrot

Seed-eating birds

Many seed eaters also eat insects

Sparrow

Dabbling birds

Duck

Meat-eating birds

Hawk

Digging birds

Sandpiper

Birds of prey have strong hooks on the ends of their beaks for pulling apart the animals they eat.

Ducks have beaks for "dabbling." They open and shut their beaks as they move their beaks through water. Their beaks are like strainers—anything that isn't water is strained out and swallowed.

Some birds have long skinny beaks so they can reach into places for food that other birds can't reach. Sandpipers live on ocean shores and can reach deep into the sand for worms.

Bird Talk

Birds use their voices for many reasons. Male birds sing songs in the spring when they are looking for female birds. The love song they sing often alerts other birds that a territory for building a nest is already claimed.

Birds sing out to each other when they see an enemy. Have you ever come near a tree where a crow is perched and found you've been announced to all the birds and other animals near the tree?

Geese honk to each other as they fly south in the fall or north in the spring.

Birds start to use their voices even when they are barely out of the egg. People sometimes complain about the terrible racket under their windows if birds build a nest and raise a family there!

Body Language

Birds also use their bodies to "talk" to each other. We usually think about language as something we can speak and hear. Maybe that's why, until recently, scientists gave more attention to bird songs than to other kinds of bird "talk."

A man named Konrad Lorenz was one of the first scientists to begin to watch how birds talk to each other with their bodies as well as their voices. He spent many years watching geese. He learned, for example, that when a goose walks toward another goose with its head stretched out front, the goose is threatening the other goose and may attack. In fact, geese may have many ways of deciding who is "top goose" in which they "talk" with their bodies but rarely fight each other.

Different kinds of birds have different ways of talking to each other with their bodies. We still have a lot to learn about bird language. You can be like Dr. Lorenz and watch a particular bird and how it talks to other birds. You may very well learn something about that bird that no one else would know! All you need is patience and the imagination to guess what the bird you are watching might be saying.

These two geese are deciding who is "top goose."

Taking a Nest

You can take a really close look at birds' nests in the fall. After the leaves have fallen, you can easily see small nests that have probably been abandoned. Many birds fly south in the winter, because they know the cold and the snow will make finding food impossible. They leave their summer nests behind.

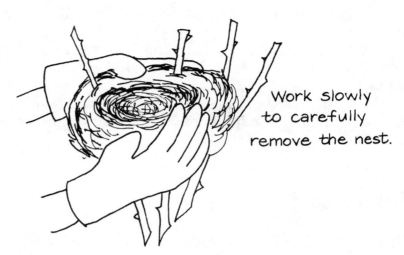

Work slowly to carefully remove the nest.

You will want to be certain, though, that the birds will no longer need the nest. Here are two rules to help you be sure the nest is no longer needed by the birds:

1. Watch the nest for a few days. If you see any birds coming and going, don't disturb it!

2. Be sure the nest won't be used next year. How can you know that? Generally speaking, larger birds who nest in trees, holes, or under the eves of houses will return and rebuild their nests. But the smaller birds, who build their nests in shrubs or bushes, will use their nests for only one year. Luckily, these are the ones that are easiest to reach, too.

How to Take the Nest

Once you know that the nest is abandoned, you can take it home with you so that you can look at it more carefully.

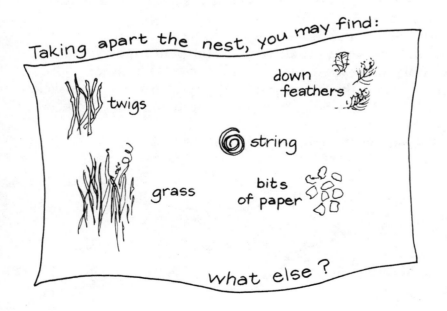

Taking apart the nest, you may find:
twigs
down feathers
string
grass
bits of paper
what else?

You need:

1. Gloves to protect your hands from the fleas that may still live in the nest

2. An adult with clippers or pruning shears

3. A plastic bag big enough to hold the nest and some of the branches it's attached to

4. Big sheet of white paper

5. Table fork or pair of tweezers

Often nests are built in dense parts of shrubs to give the bird family lots of protection. To take away the whole nest, you may need to cut away part of the shrub or bush. After you find the nest, show it to an adult, and if it's okay with him or her, ask the adult to clip out the nest by cutting all the branches that support the nest.

Wearing the gloves, take the nest and branches from the shrub. Work slowly and wiggle the nest a little if you have to.

Take Apart the Nest

Now you can find the answer to the question, "How **do** baby birds stay warm and dry in a house made of just grass and twigs?"

Spread out a big sheet of white paper so you can see everything easily. Still wearing your gloves, take apart the nest slowly, starting from the inside. A table fork may be useful, or a pair of tweezers.

Here are some questions to help you when you think about the nest and the baby birds.

- Where did you find the nest? Would you have been able to see it in the summer if you were just walking by?

- How did the inside of the nest get to be that shape?

- What kind of materials did the birds use to make the nest? Lay them out on the paper carefully in different piles, so you can look at them and think about them later.

- Are there different layers in the way the nest is built? If there are, how would you describe them?

- Pretend you are a baby bird for just a moment. What would you feel against your skin when you were in the nest?

Migration

Do you think a bird could make those amazingly long journeys in the spring and fall without feathers?

Maybe you can name some birds that migrate north in the spring and south in the fall. Maybe you are lucky enough to live under a flyway, a sort of path in the air that birds use each season they migrate. There are many routes that birds use.

Flying for Food

Picture this: There is a land that is alive with fish, berries, plants, and many insects. If you are a hawk or an eagle, there are lots of mice and other rodents to eat.

This land has all you need to live and raise a family. But there is only one problem. The land is rich with food for only part of the year. The rest of the year it is covered with snow and ice, and there is no way for you to live on that land during the cold time.

If you were a bird, what would you do?

You probably wouldn't let that chance for good living go by. You would spend the

An albatross knows the shape of her nesting island.

where there is plenty of food for them and their families.

Finding the Way

You may have heard that the same birds often return to the same nesting place year after year. The earth is a very big place! How can birds fly thousands of miles and return to the very same spot each year? Sometimes we even get lost in department stores!

Ornithologists, the scientists who study birds, haven't completely figured out the answer to that question. Here are some of the ways they think that birds might be able to find their routes to their winter and summer homes.

summer in the north country, and then go south, where you know there is plenty of good food for you to eat while the snow piles up in the north.

What would happen if birds weren't able to migrate? There would be fewer birds, and many fewer kinds of birds, in the world. Lots of birds living in just one place all the time would quickly eat up all there is to eat and then die of starvation. With migration, birds can fly over the whole earth (and some do!) to find places

Landmarks

Some birds are able to use landmarks, just the way you do. Are there places you know how to get to, but don't know the names of the streets on the way? You use landmarks. "The grocery store is on the same street as the big toy store," you may tell someone.

Sea birds like albatrosses and sea gulls can recognize the shape of the island where they nest, even from very high up.

Using the sun by day

The Sun and the Stars

Scientists know that some birds know where they are by looking at the position of the sun or the stars. People use the sun and the stars to find where they are and where the nearest land is when they are at sea.

It is very possible that some birds use the sun and the stars in the same way that sailors on the ocean do. Birds may, for example, be able to find the North Star. They then will know in which direction to fly to get to their winter or summer home.

Other Possibilities

Some birds seem able to find their way south or north by using direction finders that scientists can only guess at.

For example, the earth has a magnetic field that we can't sense, but some birds can. These birds use the magnetic field to find their north and south directions. Scientists have a lot to learn about how this works.

Birds who live on the ocean coasts or islands, scientists think, may be able to find their homes by listening for the special sounds that ocean waves make when they reach the shore of their homes. If you are ever near an ocean, you can hear for yourself that waves sound different when they break against cliffs than when they break against an open shore.

Putting It Together

A bird finds his or her way home in the spring or fall using several of the ways just discussed to find direction. Landmarks or the sun or stars are useful except during foggy or cloudy weather. But birds migrate during that kind of weather too, so perhaps they use the earth's magnetic field then. Or perhaps they know where they are by the way the air smells or from the sounds that come up to them as they fly. Or perhaps they use other direction finders that we know nothing about.

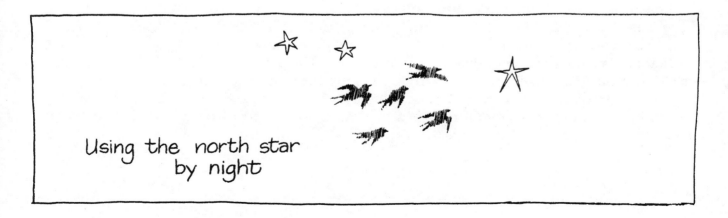

Using the north star by night

Four ways people count migrating birds and see where they go

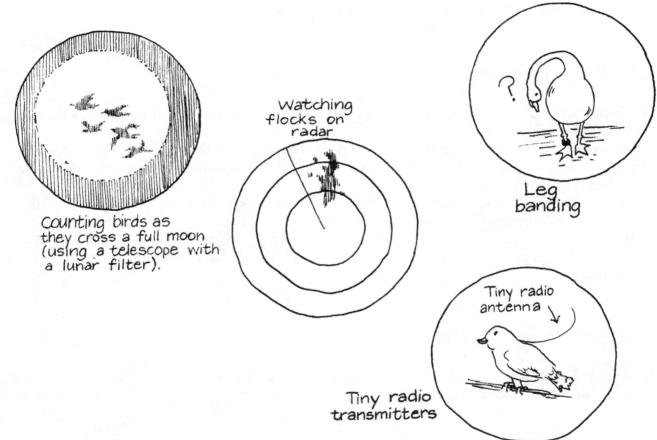

Counting birds as they cross a full moon (using a telescope with a lunar filter).

Watching flocks on radar

Leg banding

Tiny radio antenna

Tiny radio transmitters

There is a lot to learn about how birds migrate.

Learning more about bird migration may give human beings a better understanding of the complicated and beautiful way that the earth, the air, the stars, and the sun fit together. Perhaps you will be a person who increases our understanding.

Scientists often use complicated instruments to learn about birds. But the best way to learn about birds is something you can do the next time you see a bird. Just pin your imagination to the next sparrow, pigeon, bluejay, or any bird you see. Look at the world through the bird's eyes. Pretend there is a tiny camera on your bird's head. The world sure looks different through a bird's eyes, doesn't it?

Help Birds Build Their Nests

You can help the birds build their nests in the spring and early summer. Collect pieces of cotton thread or string, wool yarn, and even hair from your family's hairbrushes. Wind the materials around pine cones and tie the pine cones onto tree branches, or just stick the materials into the crooks of trees. And don't forget to put out a saucer of mud for "glue" for the birds' nests! Then watch the birds make their new homes.

Draw a flying bird!

When you draw pictures, have you ever wished that you could draw a bird so it looks like it's really flying?

You probably know about drawing birds this way. → That's a good way to show birds flying from a long way away.

Here's another way to show a flying bird, close-up. ←

It's easy!

A triangle ↓
↑And
two eggs

Draw the bird's body first

Fill in and draw a beak and tail.

Two more triangles make flying wings

You can play with the triangle wings to show different wing positions. Do you see the triangle shapes in the birds' wings at the top of the page?

How to help out backyard birds

You can help feed the birds without buying fancy bird-feeders. Here are some ideas.

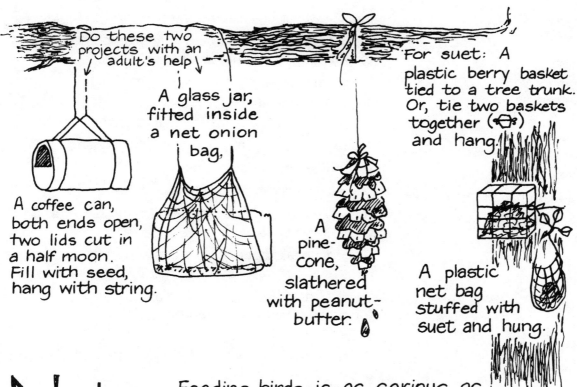

Do these two projects with an adult's help

A coffee can, both ends open, two lids cut in a half moon. Fill with seed, hang with string.

A glass jar, fitted inside a net onion bag.

A pine-cone, slathered with peanut-butter.

For suet: A plastic berry basket tied to a tree trunk. Or, tie two baskets together (⊟) and hang.

A plastic net bag stuffed with suet and hung.

Note:
Feeding birds is as serious as having a pet. Once you begin feeding them, they will die if you stop, especially in the winter.

Help the Word Bird on the Opposite Page Keep Flying!

Many water birds, when they molt, lose lots of feathers all at once. They can find safe places on the water to rest until their new feathers grow in again and they are able to fly.

But many of the birds who live on the land have to be able to fly even when they are molting. So they lose their feathers more slowly and in a special pattern. If, for example, they lose the primary feather on the tip of one wing, they will lose their exact opposite on the tip of the other wing at the same time. That way, they are still able to fly, even though they are losing many old feathers and waiting for new ones to grow in.

Help this land bird keep on flying! For every feather she loses on one side of her wing or tail, she must lose its opposite on the other wing or on the opposite side of her tail.

Write the numbers 1 through 11 on your own paper. Match the word (capital letters A through L) with the definition (write the small letters "a" through "m" on your own paper). The first one is done for you. Answers are upside down at the bottom of the page.

A. molting
B. feathers
C. barbule
D. preening
E. air foil
F. shaft
G. dabble
H. woodpeckers
I. Konrad Lorenz
J. ornithologist
K. migration
L. talons

1. ___D___ Birds use their beaks to do this frequently.

2. ___?___ A scientist who studied geese and learned how they "talk" to each other with their bodies.

3. ___?___ Hawks and other birds of prey have strong _____, or claws, to carry their prey with.

4. ___?___ When a bird sheds old feathers and grows new ones.

5. ___?___ A bird's wing is in this shape; so is an airplane's wing.

6. ___?___ A scientist who studies birds.

7. ___?___ Many animals can fly, but only birds have these.

8. ___?___ A part of the feather that grows from the barb and ends with a tiny hook.

9. ___?___ A special beak shape helps ducks and other kinds of water birds to strain water and get their food this way.

10. ___?___ These birds have two hind toes and two front toes, good for gripping tree bark when they drill with pointed beaks to get insects.

11. ___?___ A long journey many birds make to find food in the winter and the summer.

12. ___?___ The hollow tube in the center of a bird's feather.

118

CHAPTER 6

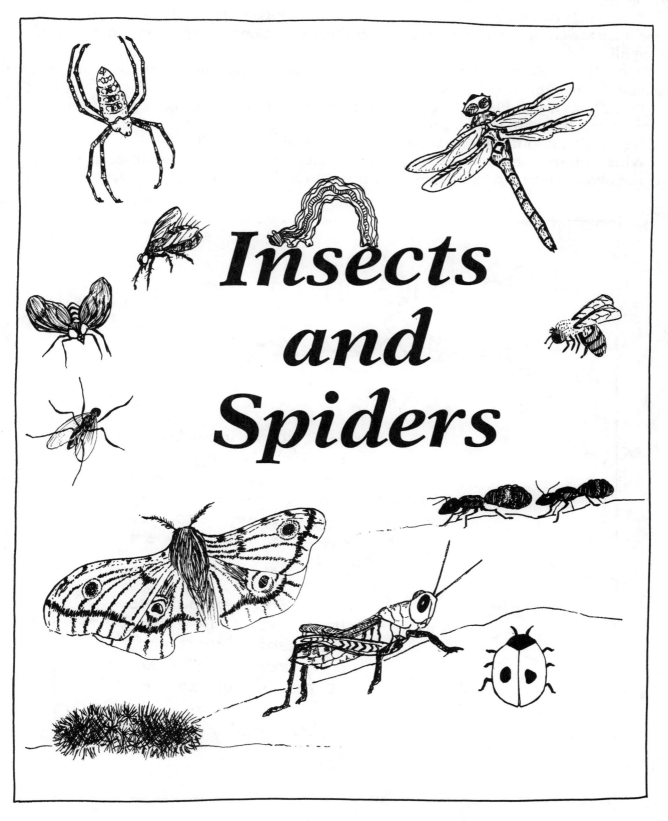

Insects and Spiders

Bugs are all the same . . . or are they? They all have six legs, right? Spiders are just like bugs, too, except they have eight legs. And many kinds of bugs have blood that's a kind of light green.

Some bugs can see even more colors than the colors in the rainbow we can see. And some bugs are completely blind, but can feel tiny vibrations in the ground that we can't feel at all.

Some bugs can smell each other from a few miles away. Some bugs have ears on their legs, and some bugs can walk on water.

Some bugs are as fierce as tigers and eat only meat. And some bugs grow fungus in underground "farms" just like people do.

Hey, wait a minute! Maybe all bugs aren't the same after all!

When you read this chapter, you will find out more about all these insects. You can find out about spiders in "Some Favorite Bugs" in the second half of this chapter.

Do bugs in the house Bug you?

Some insects just don't belong in houses. But maybe you don't want to kill them. Here's a way to remove them so you're safe and they can have a happy life outside where they belong.

Plastic cup

After you put the cup over the bug, slip an index card or cardboard gently underneath. Then let the bug go outside.

How Are Insects Alike?

If you were a scientist who studies insects, called an **entomologist**, and you found an entirely new insect one day in your back yard, how would you know it was an insect?

Even though you aren't a famous scientist right now, you already know part of that answer: an insect has six legs.

Insects are alike in their general structure, too. If you look closely at any adult insect you find, you will see the three main body parts that are in the drawing. Even insects that don't look anything like the drawing, like beetles or praying mantises, will have them and you can see them if you look closely enough.

So if you were a famous entomologist, you could count your creature's legs and look at its body parts.

There is a third thing that all insects have in common, too. It is their **exoskeleton**.

You probably know that the reason you are able to stand and run and jump is because of the hard skeleton that is inside you. You might look and move like a jellyfish without one!

Insects have skeletons, too, but they are outside of their bodies. They are made of **chitin** instead of bone. Chitin is lighter than bone, but quite strong.

Molting

Exoskeletons made of chitin can be quite a problem as an insect grows. The chitin won't grow along with the insect like your bones grow with you. When your clothes get too short and too tight, you get some bigger clothes. But what does a growing insect do?

The insect grows a new exoskeleton. But first it has to split open the old one and leave it behind.

The insect doesn't have any zippers to help it, though. As you can imagine, struggling out of the old exoskeleton is a slow and careful process. The new exoskeleton underneath is soft and will harden only when it is exposed to air. If the insect tears its body in the struggle, it could bleed to death.

Once the insect is free of its old exoskeleton, it must sit and rest for a while until its new exoskeleton hardens. It also has to hide because it's easier for animals, birds, or other insects to eat it when it doesn't have its armor. When the new exoskeleton is hard, the insect is off and on its way.

The whole process of struggling out of its exoskeleton is called **molting**. All insects molt, sometimes many times in their lives.

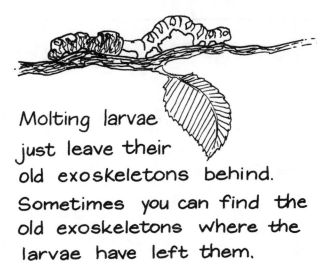

Molting larvae just leave their old exoskeletons behind. Sometimes you can find the old exoskeletons where the larvae have left them.

The main parts
of an insect's body

The insect's **head** is where the **antennae** ("feelers") are.

The **thorax** is where the insect's six legs are attached. All insects have legs with lots of joints, just like knights wearing armor do. Many insects have hooks at the ends of their legs to help them grasp the places where they stand or climb.

The **abdomen** has **spiracles**. Those are the little holes in the drawing. An insect breathes through them. An insect usually digests its food in its abdomen, and all insects need their abdomens to mate.

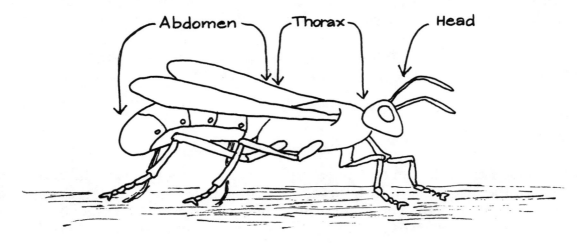

Abdomen   Thorax   Head

Do you think that you could draw any insect you wanted to, now that you know how the different parts of its body fit together?

Changing Bodies

There are two ways that insects grow from babies into adults. Each way is a type of **metamorphosis**. That is a long word that means "changing form." All insects, when they grow from eggs to adults, "change form."

One way many kinds of insects change form is called **simple metamorphosis**. Grasshoppers are a kind of insect that do this. If you were to take a photograph of a grasshopper from the time it hatched from its egg, through each molt, to adulthood, you would mostly see that the grasshopper just got bigger. Usually the only change you can see in simple metamorphosis, besides size, is that the insect grows its full-sized adult wings after the last molt. It "changes form" with each molt, but not very much.

If you live in a place with grasshoppers, sometimes you can find the exoskeletons they leave behind when they molt. Sometimes they are attached to grass or weeds. They look like little ghosts.

Complete Metamorphosis

Perhaps you already know about an insect that does a **complete metamorphosis**. Have you been lucky enough to watch a caterpillar become a butterfly or a moth?

The drawing will show you each stage of growth of an anise swallowtail butterfly.

Anise swallowtail caterpillars can eat only plants in the carrot family. You can see the adult butterflies flying around lots of places, but when it comes time to lay her eggs, the mother butterfly is careful to lay them only on Queen Anne's Lace or parsley or carrot tops growing in a garden.

Simple metamorphosis
Grasshoppers molt four or five times before they become adults.

That way the larvae will have plenty to eat as soon as they come out of their eggs. Many kinds of insects lay their eggs on or near the plants they know will nourish their young ones. Often, the parents will die before the eggs hatch, or the adults simply will not need to care for the young ones because the young ones already have all they need.

The **larvae**, or caterpillars, as we call the larvae of butterflies and moths, then start to do what the larvae of all kinds of insects do. They eat. And eat, and eat, and eat! They grow fast and molt several times.

The anise swallowtail caterpillar grows to be more than two inches long before it goes on to the next stage of complete metamorphosis.

Do you know what that next stage is? The caterpillar becomes a **pupa**. That is a resting stage, when the long, thick caterpillar slowly changes itself into a winged butterfly or moth.

For butterflies, including the swallowtail in the drawing, the caterpillar's exoskeleton becomes dry, shrunken-looking, and harder. That is when the pupa is called a **chrysalis**.

For moths and many other insects, the larvae spin a **cocoon** out of silk to protect themselves from the outside world while they change so completely.

While the insect is a pupa, inside the chrysalis or cocoon, it is doing some amazing work. What could be more different than a caterpillar compared to a butterfly? How can they be the same creature? But they are. The insect breaks down its old body and builds up its new body with wings.

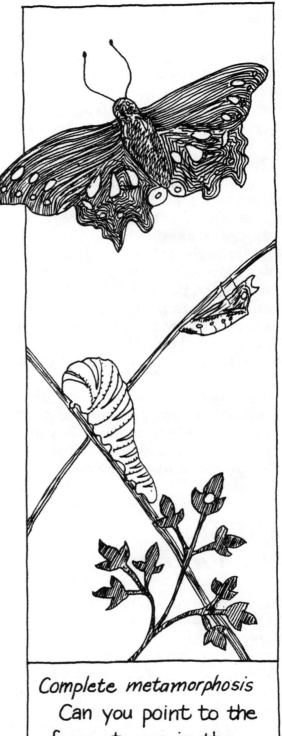

Complete metamorphosis
Can you point to the four stages in the life of this anise swallowtail butterfly?

Grown Up at Last

The butterfly has completely remade itself inside the pupa. It has turned from a caterpillar that inches along plant leaves into a butterfly that is tightly packed inside a chrysalis. And now it is time to break free!

It has to break free slowly. Any sudden movement could tear its fragile new body. After it is completely free of its new chrysalis, the butterfly must rest and let its wings fill slowly with blood to make them stiff enough for flying. After the wings are stiff and dry, the butterfly is ready to fly off, to enjoy its new life as a creature with beautiful wings.

Growing Up Weird

Whether an insect's metamorphosis is simple or complete, most people agree that insects grow up in a way that's different from human beings.

What would it be like if you grew up with two completely different kinds of bodies, one inside the other? Some insects that do a complete metamorphosis are like that. When the larva hatches from the egg, it may look long and kind of like a worm. But inside it in a very simple form are the wings, head, thorax, and abdomen it will need as an adult.

Human beings certainly don't grow that way! Have you ever looked at photographs of your parents when they were children? Can you sort of tell from the pictures taken then that they would grow up to look like they do now?

Imagine a swallowtail butterfly's family album. "No, that pupa just doesn't look a thing like you!" A grown-up butterfly might say that to another butterfly if they could talk, don't you think?

"Yetch"?

Some people think that because insects are so different from us they are ugly, or creatures to be afraid of, or just not worth the time to learn about. "YETCH," they say. "A BUG!"

But maybe getting to know creatures so different from ourselves can help us to

A butterfly pupa doesn't look at all like a grown-up butterfly.

see the world through their eyes, ears, noses, and skins. Do insects have the same senses as we do? Well, yes and no.

Insect Senses

Human beings throughout the whole world have their five senses. Whether they live in the cities, the towns, or the country, in the desert or next to a swamp, you know that most people can see, hear, taste, smell, and sense hot and cold, and touch through their skins.

You can't say the same thing about insects. They are much like the plants you learned about in Chapter 2 on green plants. They have different kinds of senses according to the kind of environment in which they live. They are **adapted** to where they live.

So insects that live in deep grasses have different needs than insects that spend a lot of time flying through the air. Insects that hunt other insects for food need senses different from insects that get their food from flowers. And insects have all kinds of ways to find each other when it comes time for them to mate and make eggs.

Insect Eyes

Have you ever wondered if you could discover a new color? You know about the colors of the rainbow. What if you could discover a color that no one has ever seen before?

Some insects see colors that we simply cannot see. They can see many of the colors that we can see, too. Bees and wasps can see all the colors we can (except red) plus some others that we can't see.

What would a bee's painting of a daisy look like? We'll never know. Not only because bees can't paint, but also because our eyes just can't see colors the same way a bee's do.

Some insects also see light in a way very different from ours. As you move your eyes toward the place in the sky where the sun is, the sky is about the same color until you get close to the sun.

Some insects see the sky very differently because of the way they see light. These insects (as near as we can

guess) see the sun's light as a series of ribbons. Scientists tell us that these insects know *exactly* where the sun is in the sky, even on a cloudy day.

Knowing the sun's exact position is important to a bee that wants to tell other bees where good nectar is to be found. You can find out more about bees in the "Some Favorite Bugs" section of this chapter.

There are a few kinds of insects, though, that have no need for any kind of eyesight. Some termites that live in the ground all their lives are completely blind. And insects that live in deep grasses all their lives don't need to see great distances through the air, so their eyesight isn't as sharp as an insect's that can expect at any minute to eat or be eaten in the air.

Big Eyes

Who has bigger eyes, a grasshopper that lives in the weeds all its life, or a dragonfly that hunts for mosquitoes for dinner in the air over a swamp?

Grasshopper's eyes look like they fit neatly into a grasshopper's head. They don't look particularly large for an insect's eyes. Since grasshoppers spend most of their time in a shady forest of grass and weeds, they don't need to see much further than a few inches away.

Dragonflies have very big eyes. They have to, because they have to see tiny mosquitoes flying through the air a long way away.

When a dragonfly sees a mosquito flying around, it doesn't see just one mosquito, the way we do. The mosquito shape is broken up into many pieces, but each piece is *moving*. The dragonfly's eyes are especially good at spotting moving insects against a background of trees and water that doesn't move very much.

Insect Ears

Sound makes waves in the air much like wind makes waves in water, only you can't see sound waves. Since you can't see sound waves, you have to imagine them.

This may help: Have you ever been inside a boat and heard the waves hit the side of the boat? You can hear even the little waves.

Inside your ear you have **eardrums**. When the sound waves hit them, you hear the sound. The boat is like an eardrum. When the waves of water touch the side of the boat, you hear the splash against the boat. When soundwaves touch an eardrum, you hear the "splash" they make against your eardrum.

Sound makes waves in air much like wind makes waves in water.

Some insects have "drums" too. They are even called a word that means "drum"—**tympanum**—but they have these drums in unexpected places.

Some kinds of grasshoppers and cicadas have these drums on their forelegs (the first pair of legs down from the head) and their abdomens. What would it be like if your ears were on your legs instead of on your head?

These insects need to be able to hear the love songs that their fellow insects are singing. If they are female, they need to know where the males are. If they are males, they still need to know where the other males are. That way they can stay out of each other's territories!

Insect Noses

Insects don't have noses like we do. Instead, they use their feelers (antennae) to smell things. They can smell lots of things with their antennae that we can't.

One difference you can easily see between butterflies and moths is that the moths have feathery antennae. Some kinds of moths, especially male moths, have very feathery antennae indeed. That is because they use their antennae to smell female moths, sometimes from several miles away.

The female moth, when she is ready to mate, puts a special smell into the air. You can't smell it, but a moth who wants to mate with her sure does! Look at the drawing to see how a male moth finds a female moth.

Many moths use the "noses" in their antennae to smell for good places to eat or to lay their eggs, as well as to find their mates.

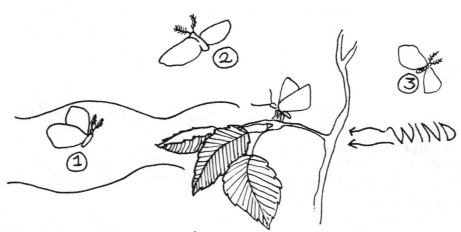

The female moth has released her scent into the wind. But if you're a male moth, you have to be in the right place at the right time. Do you think moths 2 and 3 can smell the female's scent?

Vibrations

You have probably noticed that when somebody jumps really hard in a room or when a big truck drives by, you can feel the vibration through your feet.

Vibrations can be very, very tiny too. So tiny that you wouldn't notice them, but some kinds of insects would. They use those tiny vibrations to talk to each other. Some termites in a nest (built kind of like a human apartment building) are able to feel termites below them who bump their heads into the ceilings of the nest. They feel them through tiny hairs on their legs.

Feeling that teeny tiny head bump below them is important to the termites, because head bumps are one of the few ways they can signal danger to the nest. Aren't you glad you don't have to bump your head on the ceiling just to get someone's attention?

Water striders are another kind of insect with the ability to feel vibrations through their legs. Maybe you have seen them on streams or ponds. They look like they can walk on water, and they can! They are so light that they can walk on the "skin" on top of the water that you can feel sometimes if you put your finger very slowly into a glass of water. Other insects that land on the water make tiny vibrations as they move. The water strider senses them with its legs, bounds over, and makes its meal.

Air Currents

Have you ever wondered why earwigs, crickets, or cockroaches seem to know that you are about to catch them, even though you have been completely still until the moment you move?

These insects are able to sense the tiniest puff of air, and then react very quickly. How do they sense the air your hand moves just as you strike? You can see the two parts of their bodies that tell them. They look like little tails and are called **cerci**.

Other insects can sense air currents through the hairs on their bodies or antennae. That's why it is so hard to surprise a fly.

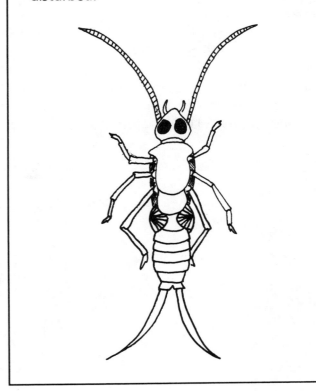

Earwigs

Earwigs certainly look scary, especially if you see them in your house. But their wicked-looking "pinchers" are really *cerci*, which sense the tiniest movement of air.

This is a female. The male is even scarier looking. His cerci have "teeth." But any earwig will just scuttle away if disturbed.

Insects and Spiders

Catching them

Read about each method and decide what's right for you and the insects you want to catch.

1. Pitfall trap.

This works best for insects who scurry on the ground.
Make a pitfall trap by burying a mayonnaise-sized jar up to its neck in a place you know lots of ground-scurrying insects will be.

Cover the jar with a piece of wood or a stone to protect it from the rain and from animals who eat insects. Set the cover on four stones to keep it about an inch above the ground.

Bait the trap at different times with different baits—meat, overripe fruit, cheese. Are your visitors different with different kinds of bait?

Check the trap *frequently*. You don't want any insects to die in there!

And ALWAYS LOOK before you reach inside.

2. Cup-and-card.

This method is good for insects that are resting on trees, houses, etc.
You can do this inside, too! Read how on page 122.

3. Shake a bush.

This is good for insects who hide in bushes.

To collect insects from a bush, place an open umbrella underneath the bush. Shake the bush or beat it (gently) with a stick. What falls out of the bush?

You may want to use a cup and card to collect the insects from the umbrella.

4. Stretch a sheet.

This method is good for insects who are active at night.

Stretch a sheet from a tree limb to the ground. At the top, tie the sheet corners to the limb with string. At the bottom, tie the sheet with string to stakes you have driven into the ground. An adult can help you reach the tree limb and put in the stakes.

Shine a flashlight behind the sheet, as shown in the drawing. Use a cup and card to collect the insects.

Insects and Spiders

Keeping them

Want to look at an insect up close?
Here are some ideas for temporary houses.

Cheesecloth or
netting tied
around a
twig
outside

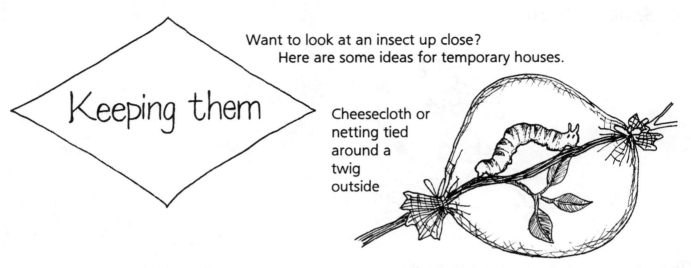

You can keep insects a few hours or overnight so you can look at them better. Give your temporary pet leaves to chew on or small insects to eat from the place where you found it. Include a twig or two for your visitor to stand on.

If you want to keep your pet for a longer time, you will need to know more about what it needs to live. Libraries can be good places to find out more about your pet.

Large jar covered with cheesecloth or netting

Hurricane lamp in sand-filled flowerpot covered with cheesecloth or netting

Hedgehog gall

Oak apple gall

Some Gall!!

Sycamore galls

Goldenrod ball gall

Many insects make homes for their little ones to grow up in. The mother adult insect lays her eggs on the leaves or stem of the kind of plant she knows her larvae will need to eat.

When the larvae hatch, chemicals on their bodies make the plant actually change its normal growth. The plant grows over the larvae, protecting them until it's time for them to grow into adults.

The larvae inside have a cozy house to live in that they can also eat up as they need to. This house is called a **gall**. Do you think it might be kind of like living in a gingerbread house?

When you are on a walk sometime, ask an adult to cut open a gall so you can look inside. Find a gall with holes in it—that means the occupants have left, so you won't be killing any living creatures when the gall is cut open.

Were the larvae safe inside? Can you see any sign that more than one kind of larvae was inside? Is there just one exit hole, or more than one?

Some Favorite Bugs

Here are just a few favorite and well-known bugs. If your favorites aren't here, or you would like to know more, libraries have some really great books about insects. Sometimes you can find books about just one kind of insect, like ladybugs. Sometimes you can find books about insects as a group.

You can learn a lot just by looking at pictures and reading the sentences about the pictures, even in books that are supposed to be for adults. Give it a try!

Spiders

 Even though we think of them as bugs, spiders are not really "insects," because they have eight legs, not six. Insects also have three main body parts, while spiders have only two. The drawing shows you an example of a spider and its main body parts.

Spiders hatch from eggs as tiny spiders. They undergo a simple metamorphosis. They molt just as insects do and can grow new legs with a new molt if they have lost them.

Many kinds of spiders have eight pairs of eyes at the front of their heads, although some kinds of spiders have fewer. The way a spider's eyes are arranged on its head can help in identifying what kind of spider he or she is.

A spider's jaws are underneath its eyes. At the tip of its jaws are "fangs" that have openings for the spider's poison, which it uses to make its prey quiet enough to eat.

Spiders mostly eat liquid food. The poison they use to subdue their insect prey also turns the insect's insides into a liquid. The spider then sucks its dinner out from inside the insect's exoskeleton almost as if it is using a straw.

At the tip of a spider's **abdomen** are six **spinnerets**. Silk comes out of them as a liquid. But it hardens almost instantly, so the spider can spin a web.

Not all spiders spin webs. Some hunt on the ground and never need a web, but they may still use silk to wrap their eggs. Spiders that do make webs make different kinds according to the kind of spiders they are.

Three kinds of web~weavers

Orb Web Weavers

Maybe you have seen garden spiders' webs on dewy mornings. They always find the best places for the breeze to bring them their breakfasts!

Funnel Web Weavers

They build "trip wires" into their webs. When their prey (often ants) trips the wire, they dash out of their funnels and pounce. Look for these webs among dead leaves on the ground.

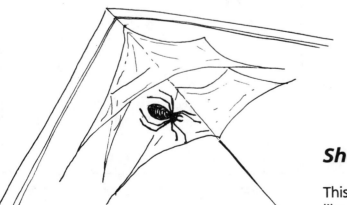

Sheet Web Weavers

This is a house spider with her web. These spiders like dark corners in houses. They can catch lots of insects, which then won't bother you!

The main parts of a spider's body

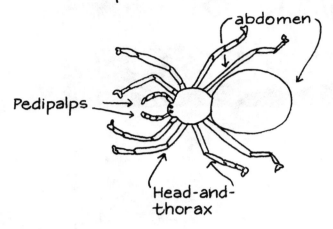

abdomen

Pedipalps →

Head-and-thorax

The spider's eyes and jaws are on its **head-and-thorax**. The spider's legs are attached here too.

The **pedipalps** are not antennae. They look a little like legs, and the spider uses them for catching the insects it eats. Male spiders have little knobs on the ends of their pedipalps that they use for mating. This is a male spider.

The spider's **abdomen** is for breathing, digesting its food, and for mating. The **spinnerets**, for making silk, are underneath the abdomen.

Ladybugs

Scientists can often tell what kinds of ladybugs they are looking at by counting the spots on their wings. "There is a seven-spot," they will say. Or "Take a look at this fourteen-spot!"

Ladybugs go through a complete metamorphosis. Ladybug larvae and adults are much loved by farmers and gardeners because they eat many insects that eat plants, aphids especially. If a gardener doesn't have enough ladybugs in her garden, she can order adult ladybugs through the mail. Sometimes they go through the mail snuggled inside of pine cones!

But some ants don't like ladybugs at all, because they like aphids for a different reason. Some ants eat honeydew, a sweet liquid that aphids make. These ants will keep "herds" of aphids just as we keep herds of cows. Ants will chase away ladybug larvae or adults, or even kill them, if they come too close to their herds.

They don't kill many, though. Ladybug larvae and adults taste really awful to ants. Scientists think that some insects are "color coded." Red or orange in an insect often means "don't eat me, I taste BAD!"

Ladybugs are good aphid hunters.

Ants

There are many, many different kinds of ants. You have probably seen big ones and tiny ones, red ones and black ones. Ants live almost anywhere in the world, so they live very different lives according to their environments. But all ants have one thing in common: They never live alone.

Some ants live underground in huge nests. Some ants live in rotting logs. Some ants make ant nests above ground that look like mounds of dust. Some ants don't make nests at all, but travel (together) all their lives. Some ants grow fungus for food inside their nests and tend it carefully, just as a farmer carefully tends his fields.

Ants use chemicals to talk to each other. You use words to talk, but ants use chemicals that their bodies make. When you see one ant rub his feelers against another ant's, they are talking. Often one ant is telling the other ant where there is some food.

Ants lay scent trails to tell each other where to find food. You can learn a little about ant language by watching a line of ants moving toward some food (maybe a crumb of something sweet you have placed down for them).

Rub your finger across a place in the line where there are no ants walking. What do the ants do?

Honeybees

Honeybees are also insects that never live alone. You have probably heard that they live together in hives. And you know how important they are to the flowers of the world. Farmers pay beekeepers to take beehives into orchards and fields when

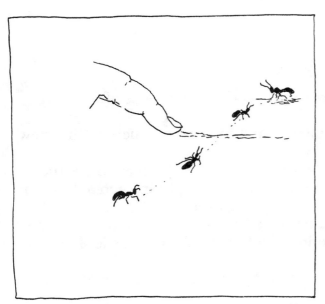

"Erase" a small part of an ant trail and watch the ants solve the problem.

Do you see this honeybee's pollen basket on her hind leg?

139

Be a Bee!

You can pollinate a flower just like a bee!

Make a bee: Take two long colored pipe cleaners (black and yellow look good) and wind them around a pencil. Leave enough of the pipe cleaners to make a good handle for your bee. Take the two ends and make antennae. Glue on some silly eyes if you want to!

Now you can take your bee to any flower you wish. Think like a bee: Where is that sweet nectar? Use the flower's honey guides (see page 31 if you don't know what honey guides are) to guide you to the nectar. "Pollination by an Insect or Animal" on page 29 shows you what happens to the flower when a bee pollinates it.

their trees and plants are blooming, so the flowers can make fruit and seeds after being visited by bees.

Did you know that bees "dance" inside their hives to tell each other where to find new places with nectar and pollen?

In their dances, they use the sun as a kind of landmark to tell each other where the flowers are blooming. They are one of the kinds of insects that see light in such a different way than we do. They can always tell exactly where the sun is, even on a cloudy day. It's something like when you tell your friend to find a treasure "twenty paces to the left of the tree," or an adult tells a driver who stops for directions that the place they are looking for is "two blocks past the dry cleaner on the corner."

Bees make the plants' nectar into honey. They also eat pollen. If you look closely, you can see the bee's pollen basket on her hind legs.

BEE PUZZLED

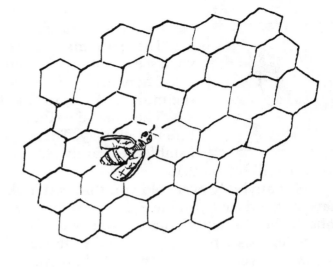

Can you make a honeycomb? Give it a try!

You need:

- two sheets of paper of contrasting colors
- a pencil
- scissors
- glue

Here is one "cell" for your honeycomb.

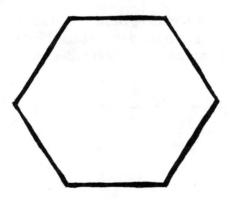

It has six sides, and people call this shape a **hexagon**. If you look at a piece of honeycomb, you will see that the bees have made it using just this one shape. One hexagon cell fits into the next hexagon cell, which fits into the next. . . .

Bees store honey in these cells, or they raise their larvae in these cells, one larva to a cell. The cells fit together like the pieces of a puzzle.

Trace the hexagon "cell" on this page. Cut out the shape and use it to trace as many "puzzle" pieces on the paper as you wish. Cut out the pieces and fit them together to make your honeycomb. You have to place them together in a certain way to fit them together properly. Can you solve the puzzle?

After you have finished, draw a bee or two or three in the honeycomb.

Flies

Next to bees, flies are the most important insect for pollinating flowers. There are many different kinds of flies besides the ones you often wish were not inside your house.

There are beeflies, which are striped like bees and stay so still in the middle of the air that they look like they are hanging from a string.

There are deerflies, which look beautiful, especially their eyes, but bite ferociously. There are stableflies that look like houseflies but bite. (Stableflies rarely get into houses, so don't worry that every housefly you see will bite you.)

Has anybody ever told you that you look just like one of your parents? Maybe you have noticed that you have, perhaps, brown eyes and your father has brown eyes, too. You inherit the characteristics of your body from your parents.

Scientists who study how inheritance works love fruit flies! They are the tiny flies you sometimes see hovering around old fruit. Fruit flies grow from egg to adult in just ten days. To study three generations of human beings (grandparents, parents, and children) would take 100 years. But for fruit flies, scientists need only 30 days.

More Flies

Some flies lay eggs on caterpillars. When the eggs hatch, the larvae have lots of food to eat—the caterpillar is breakfast, lunch, and dinner. That can be very helpful to gardeners when they have too many caterpillars eating their plants.

And don't forget that houseflies can be dangerous. Not because they bite. They don't. But they do carry the germs that can cause serious diseases in their mouths and on the sticky pads of their feet.

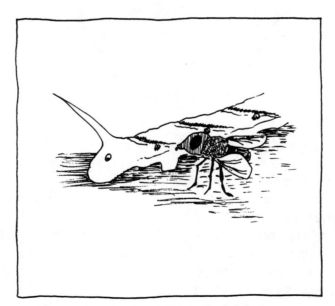

Here is a tachinid fly laying her eggs on a tomato hornworm caterpillar.

Mosquitoes

Mosquitoes are a kind of fly, too. "Mosquito" in Spanish means "little fly." Mosquitoes, like all flies, go through a complete metamorphosis. That information has been useful to people who need to get rid of mosquitoes. Many people used to die from yellow fever and malaria, diseases carried by a mosquito that likes to live in hot places.

Killing all the adult mosquitoes that fly through the air is impossible. But when mosquitoes are larvae, they live in water, so people drained swamps or covered them with thin films of oil so the larvae couldn't breathe. Now, we have medicines for those diseases.

Mosquito Bite

Perhaps you already know what is responsible for your mosquito bites. The females are the ones who make you itch! They need a meal of blood so that their eggs can develop properly.

Don't forget that many many birds, bats, and other insects need to eat mosquitoes to live. You don't have to volunteer your own blood to keep the mosquito crowd going, though. Wear long sleeves, pants, and maybe insect repellent when you know you will be outdoors with the "little flies." Native Americans used to put a thick layer of mud on during mosquito season.

Fireflies

Fireflies are insects that have excellent eyesight, especially at night. Can you guess why?

They need to see in the dark so they can find each other at mating time!

Some people wish that we could make the same kind of light that fireflies do. It is a "cold" kind of light. All the energy in the light-making process goes to light. Fireflies don't heat up the way our light bulbs do.

If you really study fireflies on a summer night, you will see that there are different rhythms in their flashes. Try imitating their flashes with a flashlight sometime. "Talk" to the firefly you are imitating and see if he answers or comes closer.

If you catch a firefly in a jar to watch its flashes up close, you may not want to keep it away from the firefly dance for too long. For only a short time on warm summer nights, fireflies must find each other, mate, and lay their eggs just below the surface of the soil.

Some kinds of fireflies' eggs, larvae, and pupae also glow with their own light. Sometimes you can find a pupa glowing in some garden soil in the spring twilight. If you are that lucky, be careful not to disturb it—it's a promise of the flashing light show to come.

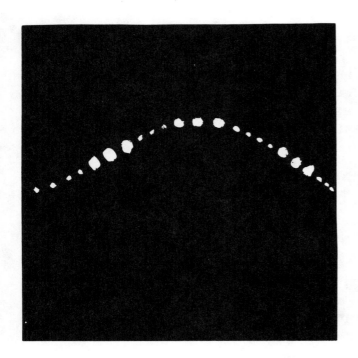

Crickets and Grasshoppers

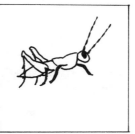

Have you ever noticed how big the hind legs of crickets and grasshoppers are? They put a lot of energy into jumping, so they need those big hind legs.

They also need big hind legs for making music. Crickets and some grasshoppers make their songs by scraping a series of ridges on one wing against a scraper on the other. Other grasshoppers rub their hind legs across a wing scraper.

You can use a comb and your fingernails or other scraper to get the same effect. Try matching your comb sounds to the rhythm of the songs you hear!

The music is usually made by males. The same song has two purposes. The first purpose is as a love song. It tells females that the males are looking for mates.

The second purpose for the songs of male crickets and grasshoppers is to keep other males away from their territories. Insects can have territories just like animals do.

It can be a lot of fun listening to the songs. Why not tune your ears to a particular song and then look for the creature who is singing it? You have to be very slow and quiet once you get close.

You can often tell if the song is made by a cricket or a grasshopper by trying to sing it yourself. If you can sing it, it is probably a cricket's song. If it sounds more like rubbing sandpaper, or scissors, it is probably a grasshopper.

Two field crickets
The cricket on the left is a female. You can tell because of her sharp-looking ovipositor. It looks like it could sting, but it doesn't. It is for laying eggs.

Then, after all that time under water, they climb above the water, shed their last exoskeleton, let their wings grow and dry in the sun, and take off. They live for only a little while as adults—long enough to eat lots of mosquitoes and to find mates and lay eggs. Then they die.

They were "children" for a lot longer than they were adults.

They have very good eyesight and are amazing fliers. People have tried to make machines that fly as well as dragonflies do. Dragonflies can hover, motionless except for their wings, then fly away so fast that you don't realize they are gone at first.

Sometimes you will see two dragonflies that look like they are stuck together. They are mating, and when they separate, the female will lay her eggs in the water or on water plants, so there will be more dragonflies next year.

Dragonflies

Do human beings spend most of their lives as children or as adults? Even though it may seem like a long time from now, you will be an adult for a lot longer than you will be a child.

Dragonflies are very different. Most kinds of dragonflies spend one or two years under water as nymphs. They go through simple metamorphosis and look much the same as adults, only smaller and without adult wings, through all their molts.

A dragonfly lays her eggs on a water plant.

Butterflies and Moths

Butterflies and moths are insects, although they don't really look like insects. A long time ago farmers called the fluttering yellow insects in their fields "butterflies" because their colors reminded the farmers of the rich, light color of butter. And the name stuck.

As you found out earlier in this chapter, butterflies and moths go through a complete metamorphosis. The caterpillars don't look a thing like the adults.

What is the difference between butterflies and moths? For one thing, most butterflies are active during the day, and most moths sleep during the day and are active at night. But that's not foolproof.

Here's the way you can really tell the difference: Look at the antennae. Moths have feathery antennae and butterflies have antennae with little knobs on the end.

Butterflies have long, hollow mouths that are curled up neatly until they drink from a flower. Then they uncurl their mouths and use their "drinking straws" to sip up nectar. It's fun to watch.

If you want to catch moths at night to look at them more closely, turn to page 133 for a way to attract them with a flashlight and a sheet.

A butterfly uncurls his tongue to sip nectar.

The Difference Between Insects and Spiders

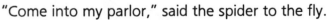

"Come into my parlor," said the spider to the fly.
"And we'll discuss our differences, the 'where,' the 'how,' the 'why.'"
"Only if you do not eat me," the fly was heard to say.
So they agreed the fly was free to fly another day.

A spider and a fly met one day to figure out how they were different and how they were the same. Here is their discussion. But they need help! They keep forgetting words.

Number your paper from 1 to 5. Every time you see a *, look at the word list and find the right word for the spider or the fly. Answers are at the bottom of the next page.

Word List

thorax
exoskeletons
abdomen
jointed
antennae

The spider and the fly looked at each other. "We look kind of the same," said the fly. "Look at our legs. Your legs and mine are both 1*, with parts that fit into each other like joints."

"Except I have eight legs and you have only six," said the spider.

"That's true. But I have three parts to my body, and you have only two. Ha!" said the fly.

"Well, wait a minute," said the spider. "You have a head. But I have a head-and-thorax. One part of my body does the work of two of your body parts!"

"True."

"You insects sense air currents, and smell each other, and touch each other with your feelers, or 2*. We spiders don't need those. We have pedipalps on our heads, to catch and crush our prey. . . . Lucky for you we agreed I wouldn't catch you today!"

"Oh, yes," said the fly in a tiny voice. He was suddenly scared.

"Don't worry," said the spider. "I just want to prove to you that I'm better looking. I have only one more body part, my 3*. Rather an elegant design, I think."

"I have one of those, too," said the fly. "Only I have a 4* in between my head and my last part. That's where my legs are attached."

"Where do you breathe?" asked the spider.

"Through my spiracles, little holes in my abdomen. How about you?"

"I have book lungs. I get all the air I need without holes. Much better, I think," said the spider.

"Hmmm."

"Hmm."

They thought for a while. Each one secretly thought he was much better than the other, but they were too polite to really argue about it.

"There is one thing we have in common," said the fly, finally.

"What's that?"

"We both have hard 5* that we need to shed when we get too big!"

They spent the rest of the conversation talking about the problems of getting out of old exoskeletons and growing new ones. They agreed that molting was a problem, but, after all, it was kind of nice to start out with a nice new exoskeleton.

"Well, see you tomorrow!" said the spider, suddenly looking hungry.

"Oh no, you won't!" said the fly. He flew away in a hurry.

Answers

1. jointed
2. antennae
3. abdomen
4. thorax
5. exoskeletons

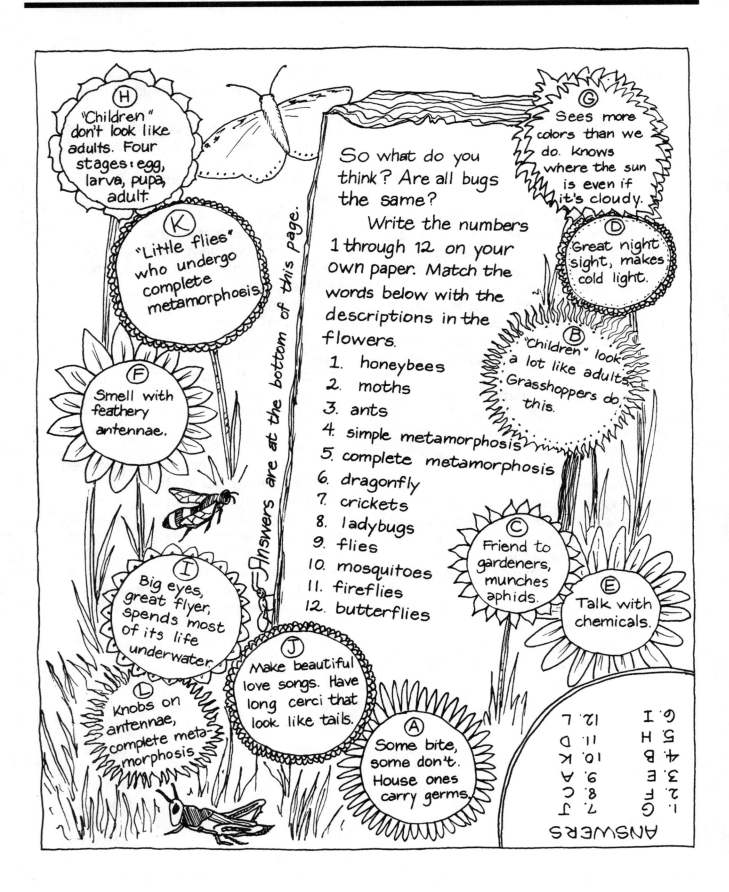

H — "Children" don't look like adults. Four stages: egg, larva, pupa, adult.

G — Sees more colors than we do. Knows where the sun is even if it's cloudy.

K — "Little flies" who undergo complete metamorphosis.

D — Great night sight, makes cold light.

B — "Children" look a lot like adults. Grasshoppers do this.

F — Smell with feathery antennae.

So what do you think? Are all bugs the same?

Write the numbers 1 through 12 on your own paper. Match the words below with the descriptions in the flowers.

1. honeybees
2. moths
3. ants
4. simple metamorphosis
5. complete metamorphosis
6. dragonfly
7. crickets
8. ladybugs
9. flies
10. mosquitoes
11. fireflies
12. butterflies

Answers are at the bottom of this page.

I — Big eyes, great flyer, spends most of its life underwater.

C — Friend to gardeners, munches aphids.

E — Talk with chemicals.

L — Knobs on antennae, complete metamorphosis.

J — Make beautiful love songs. Have long cerci that look like tails.

A — Some bite, some don't. House ones carry germs.

CHAPTER 7

Weather

It's a hot summer morning. There was no dew on the ground as the sun rose. You wander outside. You notice the screen door squeaks really loudly.

Upstairs, your mom yells at your little sister. Your dad yells at no one in particular to quiet down. And your sister yells back!

"Bad tempers," you say to yourself. But if you really think about it, your temper isn't all that great either. This morning your drawer stuck, and you pulled really hard, and the drawer came out and spilled your socks all over the floor. You weren't exactly quiet when it happened!

Outside, ants are building a tall (to them) wall around the entrance to their nest by the back door steps. A robin who usually hunts for worms on your lawn is back on her nest, even though her first family is all grown up and gone. The clover patch on your lawn has its leaves all closed up.

What *is* all this? The sun is shining. Everyone should be in a good mood. The air is hot, but the breeze feels good.

A few hours later, there's a big crackling thunderstorm. The meteorologist on the radio says a tornado has even been spotted in another county. Luckily, it doesn't go near any houses.

"That storm seemed to come out of nowhere!" a lot of people are saying. But did it really?

Weather affects birds, insects, animals, and plants. It affects screen doors, furniture, and people's moods. Sometimes we notice how weather affects us and everything that is around us, and sometimes we don't notice, perhaps because we don't know how to look. This chapter is about what makes weather change and how weather may affect animals, plants, and people.

Weather Talk

People talk about the weather in lots of ways. They can use the kinds of words you might hear on a weather report, when they see a band of clouds moving across the sky and feel a cool wind. "Here's that cold front moving in," they may say.

You have probably listened to weather reports and heard words and phrases like "warm front," "high pressure," "humidity," and "wind speed." These are words used by **meteorologists** (weather forecasters) to describe what the weather is doing.

There was a time not so long ago when there were no weather forecasters to listen to. People figured out all kinds of ways to predict what kind of weather was coming by watching the sky, watching animals' behavior, or knowing how plants change when the weather is changing. Some of these weather signs weren't very reliable. But some were accurate, and scientists now can figure out why they work.

People today sometimes still use the old ways to predict the weather. Some people use plants and animals to guess what kind of weather is coming, and sometimes people even

Old-time meteorologists

know what weather is coming from their own aches and pains. Have you ever heard an adult say, "The corns on my feet hurt. There's a storm on the way."?

In this chapter, you will learn two ways to think about the weather. The first way is the meteorologist's way, so you can listen to a weather report and better understand the big changes that happen in the sky and the air around you.

A meteorologist at work

The second way is about how you can become a weather forecaster yourself, without fancy instruments. You can learn a lot about weather changes to come by looking around at the sky, animals, plants, and even yourself.

Four Parts to Weather

Changes in the weather happen because of changes in four things: (1) air pressure (if you want to know how air can have pressure, wait until you get to the next section), (2) air temperature, (3) wind (moving air), and (4) the amount of water vapor in the air (humidity).

One day it's sunny and you feel like your sneakers have jet-packs that lift you off the ground, and the next day it rains and absolutely *nothing* goes right. The air pressure has changed.

One day you need a jacket when you're outside, the next day all you need is your shirt. The air temperature has changed.

One day it's so windy that you can fly a heavy box kite you never thought would have a strong enough breeze. The next day it's so still that smoke from a barbeque goes straight up into the sky. The speed and direction of the wind can change quickly.

And one day you wash your hair and it takes forever to dry, and the next day it dries very quickly. Humidity affects how fast things dry.

Air Pressure

You have probably heard a meteorologist or other adult talk about "high-pressure systems" and "low-pressure systems." They are talking about the pressure of the air.

How can air have pressure?

It's hard to think about, because air isn't something we can see or touch. But air is "something." It isn't "nothing." Imagine packing a large amount of air inside a pillowcase (if it was possible to do). It would be under pressure then, just like feathers are under pressure inside a pillowcase. What happens if a tightly stuffed pillow is torn? The features come spilling out, because they were packed into a tight space. Air "packed tight" is **high-pressure air**. High-pressure air is often cool and dry, and usually brings sunny weather.

Low-pressure air is like a lightly stuffed, floppy pillow with fewer feathers inside. Low-pressure air is usually warm, with water vapor mixed in, which makes it feel damp.

"Thinking About Air" on page 154 can also help you to understand how air can have pressure.

Why Isn't All Air the Same?

Why are you living in sunny, high-pressure air one day and rainy, low-pressure air the next day? Why isn't all air the same pressure?

Meteorologists know only part of the answer to that question. They do know that the place where the air comes from has a lot to do with whether it is cool and dry or warm and wet.

If air comes from a warm part of an ocean, it will be low-pressure air with lots of humidity. If air comes from the cool, dry north, it will tend to be high-pressure air. But so much can happen to the air on its way to the south or north that is sometimes difficult to understand or predict, even for a scientist.

153

Thinking About Air

You can't see the air.
You can't touch it.
But you want to *understand* it.
Air isn't "nothing."
A bottle full of air is full of "something."

When you play with a cup in the bathtub, you can hold it carefully upside down, holding the air in the cup until the cup reaches the bottom of the tub. You tip the cup a little and what happens?

Blooomp. Blooooomp.

That cup was full of *something* that bubbled up. Otherwise the water would have just rushed in and filled the cup as soon as you set it in the tub.

So. Air is SOMETHING.

You can think about air as being like tiny marbles floating around you, separated by empty space. These marbles are so tiny that scientists can't see them, even with the most powerful microscopes that have been made.

You need these tiny marbles of air to breathe. Plants need these tiny marbles to breathe, too. So do cats, dogs, and even fish, because these tiny marbles dissolve in water just like sugar does.

You just can't see all these tiny marbles.

Here is a drawing of what the air you are breathing might look like:

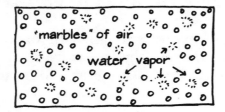

You see rain coming down one morning and sun shining the next because different air systems come and go through the place where you live.

High-pressure air brings sunny weather. Low-pressure air brings rain to clean the earth and help plants grow.

Here is a drawing of what the air might look like when a high-pressure system of air comes to where you live:

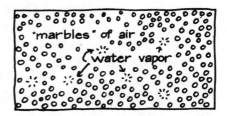

Do you see how closely packed together the marbles of air are? And you have probably noticed the water vapor mixed in. But only a little water vapor is mixed with the air. There isn't enough to make a rain cloud!

Here is a drawing of low-pressure air:

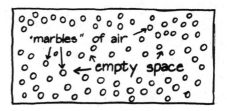

It is less tightly packed. And there is a lot more room for water vapor.

These drawings may help you when you think about air. Air looks and feels like empty space, doesn't it? But it's not.

Meteorologists know they have a lot to learn. Predicting the weather is still a hard job, because there is a lot we don't know about how air pressure, wind, temperature, and humidity come together and make weather.

Temperature

On a frosty fall morning, after the sun has been up for a few hours, the frost has disappeared everywhere except maybe under shady trees. What is the difference in the air temperature between when the frost formed and when it disappeared?

At night, when there is no sun, the air is cooler. In the daytime, the sun warms the air. Sometimes, even in the summer, when the sun goes down it is chilly enough to wear a sweater.

On the desert, it can be blazing hot during the sunny daytime and very chilly that same night. During the day, the desert soil and plants absorb the sun's heat like a sponge absorbs water. At night, the heat that the desert absorbed goes up into the night air and disappears.

No matter where you live, land and water absorb the heat of the sun during the day. At night, the heat is released into the air. On a desert, there are usually no clouds over the land to hold the heat close to the earth. (Clouds are like blankets that hold your body's heat close to you when you are in bed.) On a clear night anywhere, heat from the day will disappear into the air faster than it would if there is a cloud cover.

Temperature Changes with the Seasons

Temperatures change with the seasons, too, of course. In the summer, the sun stays in the sky longer and days are warmer. In the winter, days are shorter and colder.

Why do our seasons change so much? There is such a big difference between a hot summer and a cold winter!

To understand why seasons change, you have to picture the whole earth as a round ball, going around the sun in a circle.

The sun is round like the earth, but much, much bigger. And it is *hot*. Instead of being made of water and land, like the earth, the sun is made of fiery burning gases.

In a year's time, the earth circles around the sun once. If you picture the Arctic North Pole as

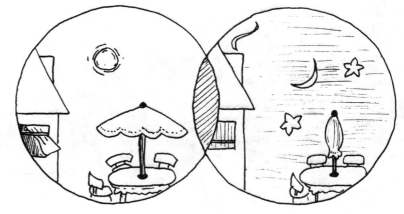

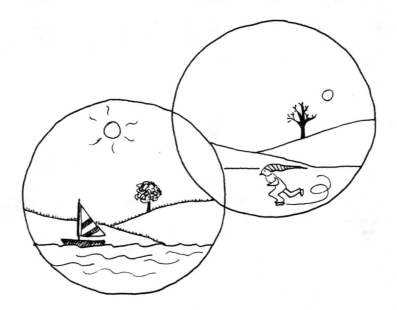

the "top" of the earth, you might say that during the warm seasons, the earth's top is tilted toward the sun.

During the cold seasons, the earth's top is tilted away from the sun (but the "bottom" of the earth, the South Pole, is then tilted *toward* the sun, so people living on the southern part of the earth have their summer).

Up north, as September turns into October, and October turns into November, days get shorter. There is less sunlight during the day, and the sun doesn't rise as high in the sky as it does in the summer. Off come the leaves from the trees, out come the birds to play in the wind, and on go the winter clothes.

Wind

Wind is moving air. Why does the air move? We know there isn't a giant person somewhere just behind the hill, cheeks puffed, blowing hard at our hats.

What makes air move? Mostly, air starts to move when warm air mixes with cool air. This is true even in the winter, because it doesn't take much of a difference in temperature for two different weather systems to meet and jostle each other around to make moving air, or wind.

Humidity Is Water Vapor in the Air

When the sun heats water in the ocean, a lake, or any body of water, some of the water **vaporizes**. Water can actually change from a liquid you could drink into a gas that you could breathe. Water from a body of water (or from damp soil, clothes drying on a clothesline, or from anything that was wet) that has vaporized and become a part of the air is called **water vapor**.

Water vapor in the air makes you feel sticky on a hot day before a thunderstorm. If there is a lot of water vapor in the air when you wash your hair, your hair will dry slowly. When there is a lot of water vapor in the air, we say the humidity is high.

The opposite of water vapor is **water condensation**. Water vapor is a gas that you can breathe. When water vapor condenses, it changes from a gas you can't see to a liquid that you can see and touch and even drink—dew. If it is very cold, it freezes into frost.

Water vapor in the air changes from vapor to dew or fog, rain or snow, frost or sleet, according to the temperature of the air. But the water vapor needs something to cling to, maybe as tiny as a grain of dust or pollen, before it becomes a form of water we can see or touch.

So, for water to condense out of the air, it needs two things: a temperature change from warmer to cooler and something to cling to.

How to

⋄Windmill⋄

You need: light-weight stiff paper about 4 inches (11 cm) square, a new pencil with a good eraser, a ruler, pencil, scissors, straight pin, and a tiny piece of paper and some tape for the "spacer bead."

1. Join opposite corners of the paper with light pencil lines, using your ruler.

2. Cut about 2¼ inches (about 6 cm) from each corner.

3. Erase the pencil lines.

4. Make a "spacer bead":
Tiny strip of paper rolled up ↗ Tiny piece of tape

5. Curl one blade toward the center as shown. Hold it down with your thumb (or a friend's thumb). Curl the remaining three blades the same way.

6. Push the straight pin through the center of the windmill through the four blades and the back. Put the "spacer bead" on the pin and push the pin into the eraser.

7. Find a puff of wind!

An adult can point out compass directions for you

Wind direction and what it means
In most of the country, wind blowing from...
the <u>west</u> brings sun; <u>east</u> means rain; <u>south</u> hot, maybe rain; and <u>north</u>, clear and cool.

Catch the wind

❖ Wind sock ❖

You **need**: an old shirt sleeve, about 18 inches (45 cm) of flexible lightweight but firm wire (ask an adult to cut it for you), needle and thread, small stone for a weight and about 1 yard (1 meter) string, scissors.

1. Cut the shirt sleeve so it is a straight tube.
2. Bend the wire into a circle to fit the widest end of the sleeve.
3. Sew the overlapping edges over the wire.
4. Bunch the bottom of the circle over the stone and sew it in (see the drawing above). This will weight your wind sock.
5. Tie the string to the place opposite the weight and tie it to a tree branch. The weight will keep the "mouth" of your sock facing into the wind.

❖ Weather vane

You **need**: a pencil, thin cardboard or index card paper, drinking straw, pencil with a good eraser on the end, scissors, straight pin.

1. Cut two slits in the straw:
2. Cut two paper or cardboard triangles as shown in the drawing. The "pointer" will be smaller.
3. Push the straight pin through the middle of the straw and into the top of the pencil eraser.

Take this outside whenever you want to know the wind direction. The arrow will point to the direction the wind is coming _from_. If the arrow points west, it is a west wind.

Make your own dew!
It's simple!

1. Take a drinking glass.

2. Fill it with ice and water.

3. Wait a few minutes. You've made your own dew!

Do you know:

The water inside the glass did not magically go to the outside of the glass. The air around the glass had water vapor in it. The ice cooled the air around the water vapor. And the glass became the "something to cling to" for the water vapor. Voilà! Condensation! Homemade dew!

Dew and Frost

Do you ever see dew forming during the day, when the sun is warming the air?

No. Dew forms only when the air cools after the sun goes down. That's the temperature change. The "something to cling to" is every blade of grass, every spider web, every leaf, your bike. . . .

If the temperature of the air goes below the temperature where water freezes, dew freezes into frost.

Rain

Chances are that at some time in your life huge gray or white objects as big as mountains and holding enough water to fill thousands and thousands of swimming pools have floated right over your head. Maybe you were inside and didn't notice them. Maybe you were outside and did notice them. Maybe you said, "That one looks like a giant monster sheep!"

Weather Facts

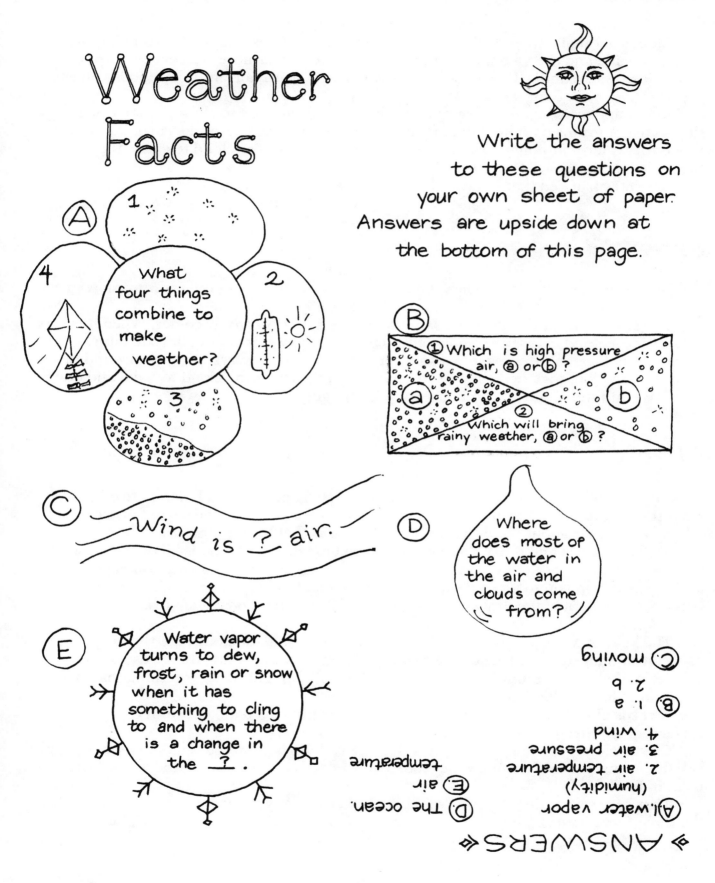

Write the answers to these questions on your own sheet of paper. Answers are upside down at the bottom of this page.

A — What four things combine to make weather? (1, 2, 3, 4)

B — ① Which is high pressure air, ⓐ or ⓑ? ② Which will bring rainy weather, ⓐ or ⓑ?

C — Wind is ? air.

D — Where does most of the water in the air and clouds come from?

E — Water vapor turns to dew, frost, rain or snow when it has something to cling to and when there is a change in the ? .

⇒ ANSWERS ⇐

A) 1. water vapor
   2. air temperature (humidity)
   3. air pressure
   4. wind

B) 1. a
   2. b

C) moving

D) The ocean.

E) air

161

If it was very gray, maybe it rained some of that water on you.

Clouds get their water from lakes and oceans, from trees and plants, from laundry drying outside and even from perspiration drying from your nose. The water **evaporates** from those places and is lifted up as water vapor with warm air until the clouds you can see from the ground form in the sky.

Rain happens when the water gets cool enough so it starts to cling to something tiny—dust or grains of pollen lifted by the wind from the surface of the earth into the air. When the water-and-pollen-or-dust drops get too heavy for the cloud to carry, they fall to the earth as rain.

Are you surprised that a raindrop isn't just water?

Snow

Just as dew freezes into frost when the air is cold enough, so rain freezes into snow inside a cloud when the inside of the cloud is cold enough.

The story of a snowflake is the same story as a raindrop's, only colder. When it is very cold inside a cloud, and there is lots of water vapor, the water vapor clings to a tiny grain of dust or pollen, and freezes into a snow crystal. When snow crystals move around inside the cloud and join together, they often become too heavy for the cloud to hold, and down they fall, onto the ground, your house, or your tongue.

Clouds

Do you remember from Chapter 4, about animals, why people find it handy to classify what they see in the natural world? Classifying clouds makes it a lot easier for people to talk to each other about the different kinds of clouds that form in the sky.

Meteorologists and other scientists may need to talk about clouds all day long, so they use a classification system with three main kinds of clouds. The drawings on pages 164 and 165 will help you to picture each of the three main kinds of clouds. They are labeled with capital letters in the drawing. Here are the three main kinds of clouds:

The kind of cloud we most often picture when we think of clouds are the big puffy cauliflower-shaped clouds. They are **cumulus** clouds, and they are often close to the surface of the earth. "Cumulus" means "heap" or "pile" in Latin. Do you think that is a good name for this kind of cloud?

Stratus clouds make the sky look like someone pulled a blanket over it (and you are underneath). "Stratus" means "stretched out" in Latin.

Cirrus clouds are the wispy clouds that are very high up in the sky. Sometimes people call them "mare's tails" because they look like a horse's tail blowing in the wind. "Cirrus" is Latin for "curl."

There are seven other kinds of clouds. They are mostly named using combinations of the three main names. They look like combinations of the three main clouds, but are at different heights in the sky. You can see them in the drawings, too. Can you find all these kinds of clouds in the sky? Do you ever see more than one kind of cloud at the same time?

Weather Signs

People who lived before weather reports (and lots of people nowadays) knew how to "read" the natural world around them. They used signs in the natural world to predict the weather sometimes hours, sometimes days, ahead of time.

You can learn how to do this, too. In fact, it's a good idea to begin to listen, smell, look, and feel for weather signs for two reasons. The first is, the weather reports you hear and see are often for large areas, and not specifically for where you are. Have you ever heard a weather report predicting rain, but not seen a drop all day? But maybe the people in the next county got rained on a lot.

The second reason to become a "natural weather forecaster" is because it is a good way to learn about all the little parts of where you live. By looking for weather signs, you begin to see how living things fit into each others' lives. When do you see birds that eat insects flying low and eating a lot of bugs? Do you get more mosquito bites before a storm? These two questions are related. The natural world is like a puzzle. Everything you learn about it has a meaning and fits into something else. What you learn about it has a meaning, and fits into something else. What you learn may not have a clear meaning right away, but it may someday, when you find another piece of the puzzle.

Clouds Predict Weather

Meteorologists look at clouds very carefully. They think that clouds are very important when they want to predict what the weather will be like.

But did you know that before there were meteorologists to give a daily weather report, many people knew how to tell what the weather might be like in a few hours just by looking at the clouds?

A cloud's shape, color, and size can tell a cloud watcher a lot about what's coming. Also, how fast the clouds move and how quickly or slowly they change shape can help a cloud watcher know what's ahead.

Have you ever seen a "thunderhead"? Then you would understand this old-time poem:

When mountains and cliffs in clouds appear,
Some sudden and violent showers are near.

Meteorologists call thunderheads **cumulonimbus** clouds. You remember that cumulus means "pile." "Nimbus" means "rain." Thunderheads often look like they are piling up.

Have you noticed how low in the sky those thunderheads are? If you were watching the sky before the thunderheads rolled in, you may have seen some **stratocumulus** clouds. They come in in the middle level of the sky. They aren't as low as thunderheads.

Clouds

CIRRUS

cirrostratus (thin white or pale gray)

Highest clouds ↑

altostratus (a gray veil, but you can still see the sun)

Stratocumulus (a little puffy, with holes to see blue sky through)

CUMULUS

Middle clouds ↑

nimbostratus (flat, dark gray rain or snow clouds)

Lowest clouds ↑

cirrocumulus
(look like ribs or
ripples)

altocumulus (patterned
clouds, often rippled)

cumulonimbus
(thunderclouds)

STRATUS

fog

DON'T
get struck by
LIGHTNING!

If indoors:

Stay away from open doors and windows. Disconnect electrical appliances. Don't use the telephone unless you have to call for help! Lightning can come in on the phone lines.

If outdoors:

If you're in a car, stay there with the windows closed.

Seek shelter: A cave (not too far in!), or a ditch or canyon away from water is good. Single trees are <u>not</u>. They attract lightning, so stay away from them.

If you're in an open field:

Crouch down, hugging your knees. Get all metal as far away from you as can — no metal umbrellas, metal frame backpacks, bicycles, farm or golf equipment allowed!

This kind of cloud can give you advance warning of thunderheads to come. If they look gray and come with a strong wind, watch out! They could bring anything from a light rain (or snow) to a big thunderstorm.

Knowing when a thunderstorm is coming is especially useful because thunderstorms can be so dangerous. You don't want to be outside in the lightning.

What are lightning and thunder? Lightning is electricity that is made when millions of tiny water drops speed around inside a cloud. The drops rub against each other and make electricity. When there is too much electricity for the cloud to contain, it bursts out and becomes lightning.

Lightning is very hot. It heats up the air around it very fast. The air expands very fast. It expands so fast that it makes a very loud noise—thunder!

More Clouds

Low, gray cumulus clouds, if they become larger and closer together, may turn into thunderheads.

Stratus clouds—which look like low, gray blankets—can bring long rains, though often they will just pass over.

You can expect rain in a few hours if you see **altocumulus** clouds. Those are little, puffy clouds that are in the middle level of the sky. They aren't really high, but aren't as low as cumulus clouds either.

Cirrocumulus clouds are very high, tiny, puffy clouds. They look like they are rippling across the sky, very high up. When you see those clouds, they tell you that a change in the weather is coming. Sailors call a sky with these high clouds that look like the scales of a fish a "mackerel sky," and they say,

Mackerel sky, mackerel sky,
Never long wet, never long dry.

Sailors long ago didn't have any weather forecasters telling them to expect constantly changing weather, but they knew what kind of weather to prepare for anyway.

Mackerel sky, mackerel sky,
Never long wet, never long dry.

Animal Forecasters

Before the weather changes, there are tiny changes in air pressure. Animals and insects sense these changes often before we do, so people have watched animals and insects for weather signs for a long time.

None of these animal forecaster tips is foolproof. But it is possible, by watching animals carefully throughout many seasons, to be able to "read" what animals are telling us about weather to come—especially storms. The secret is: Keep your eyes open.

The robin in the little story at the beginning of this chapter is a good example of an

Sometimes dogs will warn you when a storm is coming.

animal forecaster. Do you remember that the robin returned to her nest before the storm, instead of hunting for worms? Scientists guess that robins do that for two reasons. The first is that the low-pressure air that comes before a storm is harder to fly in (airplane pilots know this too). The second is that a robin's nest isn't very sturdy and needs a robin to sit in it to hold it together during a storm's high winds.

Different kinds of birds live in different places in North America. Get to know what "normal behavior" is for the birds who live near you. See if some kinds of birds make more noise before a storm, or if they become silent or even disappear. Then you can watch the birds to help you to predict what's to come.

People have noticed that animals who live in the ground often move to higher ground before a storm. Can you guess why?

You wouldn't want to live in a burrow full of water, either!

If you see mice, woodchucks, rabbits, turtles, or other ground dwellers moving suddenly, you know a whopper of a storm is coming.

If you see hawks suddenly where you haven't seen them hunting before, maybe they are hunting for the animals on the run from the storm.

You can see deer eating a lot before a long snowstorm. They know they won't be able to get food for a while.

Some pets, especially dogs, start to get jumpy before a storm. Dogs have been known to warn people that a tornado was coming their way by acting very upset before it struck.

This butterfly has found a safe place to hide from the storm.

Insects

People living with cockroaches are often not fond of them at all. They notice that cockroaches move around most at night, when it's dark. If cockroaches move around a lot in broad daylight, watch out! You may be in for a storm!

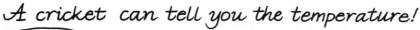

A cricket can tell you the temperature!

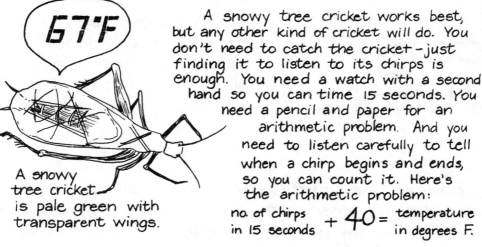

67°F

A snowy tree cricket is pale green with transparent wings.

A snowy tree cricket works best, but any other kind of cricket will do. You don't need to catch the cricket—just finding it to listen to its chirps is enough. You need a watch with a second hand so you can time 15 seconds. You need a pencil and paper for an arithmetic problem. And you need to listen carefully to tell when a chirp begins and ends, so you can count it. Here's the arithmetic problem:

$$\text{no. of chirps in 15 seconds} + 40 = \text{temperature in degrees F.}$$

Ants living in the ground build high walls around tunnel or mound entrances when they know that storms that bring flooding rain are coming.

Spiders aren't insects, but they can tell you about weather to come too. Orb web weavers take down their webs before a storm. They don't want their webs broken by wind and rain!

You can find butterflies getting safe and cosy as the skies darken. They find shelter under leaves and tree branches to wait out the storm.

Green Forecasters

Some plants can tell us about changing weather, too. Have you noticed how dandelions close up at night? They will also close up before a storm. If you notice that dandelion flowers aren't open after about eight o'clock in the morning, or if they start to close up in the middle of the day, you may soon be looking for your raincoat.

If you get to know a chicory plant, you can tell from how open or closed its blossoms are what to expect from the sky in a few hours. Sometimes you need to really get to know a plant, from watching it over several days or even weeks, to be able to learn exactly what the plant is telling you about the weather. The "Chicory Challenge" drawing will show you one way you can keep track of what the chicory is telling you.

Scientists think that many plants change because they feel tiny changes in air pressure or humidity, or both. Rhododendron plants can tell you about cold temperatures. Sure, you can just look at a thermometer. But isn't it more fun to ask a rhododendron how cold it is?

Rhododendron plants have shiny oval leaves that stay on the plant through the winter. Lots of people grow them because of their beautiful flowers in the spring. (And you know why bees love them from reading about green plants. Remember the drawing on page 31?)

Those leaves sure look different on a cold winter day! If it's cold enough for puddles to freeze, the leaves start to droop. If the temperature is at 0 degrees Farenheit (–18 degrees Celsius), the leaves will droop all the way down. They will also be tightly curled. (Rhododendron leaves also curl up in hot dry weather to keep from losing moisture.)

The Chicory Challenge

The chicory plant grows almost anywhere the soil has been disturbed – abandoned fields, roadsides, vacant lots, even sidewalk cracks in the city. You will recognize its rich blue flowers.

Choose one particular chicory plant for a friend. Visit your friend every day at the same time. Some time in the morning is best, because chicory flowers often fold up after the noon hour.

Bring a notebook with each visit. Make four columns. Here is an example:

Date	weather at 10 a.m.	flower shape	weather in afternoon
Aug. 11	mostly cloudy	☖	drizzle
Aug. 12	sunny	✳	sunny

On August 11 the flowers were almost closed at 10 a.m. On August 12 they were fully open at 10 a.m.

Do the colors of the flowers change with the weather too?

Note: This may not always "work" the way you expect — folded up flowers may mean clouds, not rain, for example. But keeping a record of changes will still help you to see the relationship between chicory and the weather.

You Are a Forecaster, Too

Just as you can observe animals, insects, and plants for weather signs, you can observe yourself and your house, too.

Do you remember that at the beginning of the chapter, in the description of what happened before the storm, the screen door squeaked really loudly? There are two reasons for the loud squeak.

The first is that wood tends to swell with increased humidity. There is more water vapor in the air, and the wood absorbs some of it. Places where wood meets wood, like where screen doors meet wooden frames, tend to get very tight. And noisy.

The second reason is because humid air carries sound better. People used to talk about a "good hearing day." If you live in a city, have you noticed how much better you hear street sounds on a hot, sticky day?

You also can smell things better before a rain. Rain comes in with low-pressure air. Low-pressure air means less weight pressing on the ground. Odors that are kept pressed down with high pressure have a chance to rise up to your nose. That is why people say they can "smell a rain coming." Can you?

Your hair changes with the amount of water vapor in the air. Curly hair gets even curlier as it absorbs water vapor. Straight hair seems to hang limp.

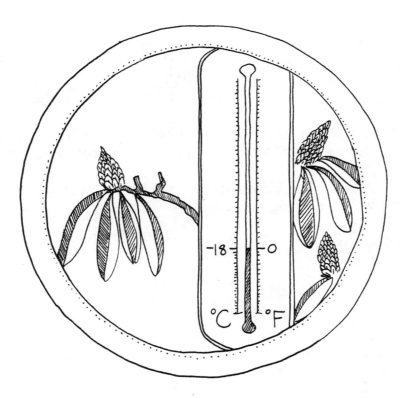

The colder it is, the more tightly curled you'll find rhododendron leaves.

Weather Walks

You can predict the weather!

Do you know the answer to the question that ends each story? Answers are upside down at the end of the last story.

A Winter Walk

You live in a city. It is winter. This morning you noticed that the sparrows you feed in the alley by your apartment building were even noisier than usual. The seed you'd left from yesterday was all gone.

You look at the rhododendron leaves by the bank building on your way to school. Its leaves are curled and drooping about halfway. "Not *too* cold," you think. "But below freezing." The air feels damp.

You can't see the sun. Stratus clouds cover it. They aren't a very dark gray, but the sky looks darker in the direction the wind is blowing from.

■ What's going to happen soon?

A Spring Walk

High up in the sky you see some cirrocumulus clouds. There is a brisk wind blowing. It's a little chilly and damp, so you put on your hat. But the sun, after a long winter, makes you want to turn a cartwheel or two.

■ What kind of weather is coming?

A Summer Walk

You live in the country. The meteorologist says to expect thunderstorms. The woodchuck who lives by your compost heap in the back yard scrambles out of his burrow and disappears into the woods on the hill.

You see a box turtle crossing the road in front of your house. Not many cars come your way, but you move her into safety anyway. A hawk circles over the north field.

"Big storm coming," you think. It's very windy, but you can still smell the cabbages your neighbor is growing.

Will it be an ordinary thunderstorm? Your dog has been running around your legs whining for the last half hour. You decide to try to convince everyone to move into the storm cellar.

■ What happens next?

An Autumn Walk

You live in a town close to a city. The sky is a brilliant blue. So are the chicory flowers. They are fully open. Fallen leaves are dry and crunch when you walk on them. There's a little breeze, not too cold, not too hot, but just right.

Your hair dried quickly this morning after your shower. "I could jump high enough to touch that branch," you think. And you do!

■ What kind of weather will be around for a while?

Don't forget that being an accurate forecaster takes lots of practice and excellent observation skills. You noticed that each story has many clues. It's a good idea to pay attention to many little details when you want to predict the weather. One little fact alone may not be accurate. So keep alert to all the ways the parts of the natural world fit into each other. Chicory flowers, cloud shapes, hungry birds, the smell of the air, and much more will tell you secrets if you listen and learn to understand them.

Answers

■ A heavy snowfall
■ Changeable—some cold spring showers, some sun
■ A tornado has formed and barely misses your house. But everyone is safe, thanks to you!
■ Clear and sunny. Enjoy it!

Human hair shrinks and expands with wet and dry weather by about two percent. That means if your hair is 100 inches long (and your name is Rapunzel!), it will shrink two inches when the weather goes from wet to dry. Human hair is so accurate that meteorologists use **hygrometers**, instruments that measure humidity in the air, that are made with one strand of human hair. They have found that blonde hair seems to work the best.

Your mood may change with the weather, too. Have you noticed that in gray, humid weather, often before a storm, sometimes nothing seems to go right? Your whole family may be a little irritable, or everyone in your classroom may be a little wild. When low pressure moves in, we often have to be a careful not to let our tempers get out of control. Human beings often seem to feel best during sunny, high-pressure weather.

People and Weather

You may have been hearing how people are worrying about forests being cut down in this country and to the south in the rain forests. People say that because of tree cutting and air pollution, the climate may be changing for the worse.

In South America, an island became a desert when trees along the coastline closest to it were cut. Rain no longer fell frequently enough, and the climate changed.

But in India, people planted trees near a place that got very little rain, and when the trees grew up, the weather changed so that enough rain fell to water the crops that the people there needed to live. And all they did to change their weather was plant trees!

Change the Weather—Plant a Tree!

If you plant a tree, can you change the weather? It won't look like it. And a lot of people may laugh at the thought that one person (especially a child) can change the world.

Maybe you know about ways you can help change the ecology. Separating trash for recycling helps. Using cloth sacks instead of plastic or paper bags at the grocery store helps. Writing letters to the people in the government helps. Planting trees helps.

But do you know what helps the most? It's very simple: Love the earth. Love trees, plants, animals, insects, and whatever weather comes your way.

You already know how to do the kind of love it takes to change the world. You have already been doing it! Always be on the lookout to learn more about the life of nature around you. Not just from books, although they help.

You learn best by sinking your toes into the ground and following your nose, your eyes, your ears, and your fingers.

Loving the earth means always learning more about it. That way, as you grow older and learn more, you will be able to think about better ways to change the way people and the earth live together.

When you were really little, you learned how to walk. Did you stop to ask what walking is for? No! You won't have to stop and ask what learning about the earth is for, either.

So go ahead—plant a tree!

An ocean of air

Some people say that the sky above us is like an ocean of air.

The ocean has currents of warm water and cool water flowing through it.

The sky has currents of warm air and cool air.

The ocean has grasses waving in the current, anchored to the bottom.

The sky has trees and bushes and flowers, waving in the breeze.

The ocean has little fish, that dart through its water.

The sky has...

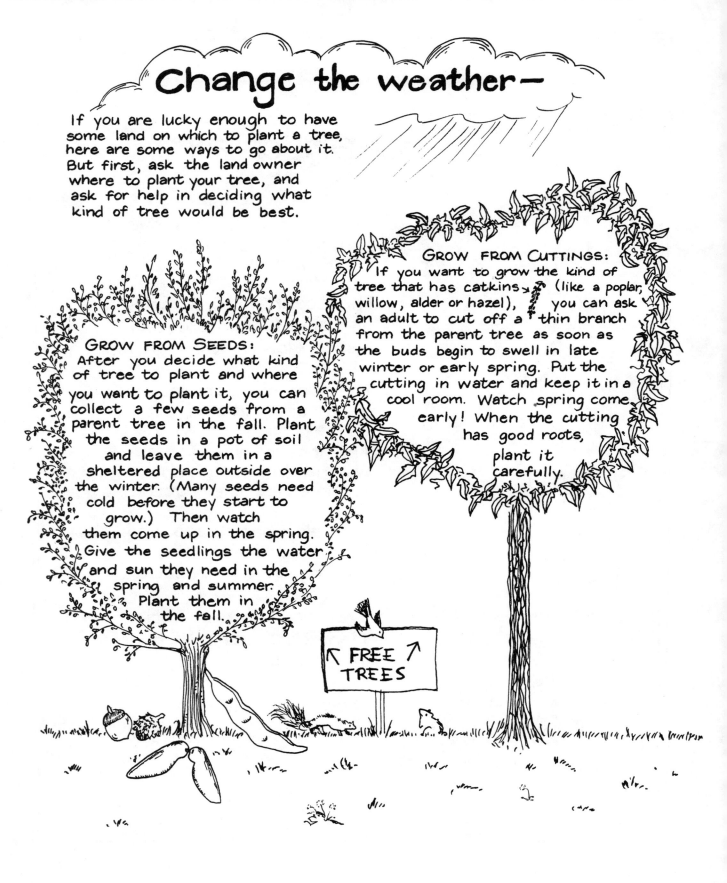

Change the weather—

If you are lucky enough to have some land on which to plant a tree, here are some ways to go about it. But first, ask the land owner where to plant your tree, and ask for help in deciding what kind of tree would be best.

GROW FROM CUTTINGS:
If you want to grow the kind of tree that has catkins (like a poplar, willow, alder or hazel), you can ask an adult to cut off a thin branch from the parent tree as soon as the buds begin to swell in late winter or early spring. Put the cutting in water and keep it in a cool room. Watch spring come early! When the cutting has good roots, plant it carefully.

GROW FROM SEEDS:
After you decide what kind of tree to plant and where you want to plant it, you can collect a few seeds from a parent tree in the fall. Plant the seeds in a pot of soil and leave them in a sheltered place outside over the winter. (Many seeds need cold before they start to grow.) Then watch them come up in the spring. Give the seedlings the water and sun they need in the spring and summer. Plant them in the fall.

FREE TREES

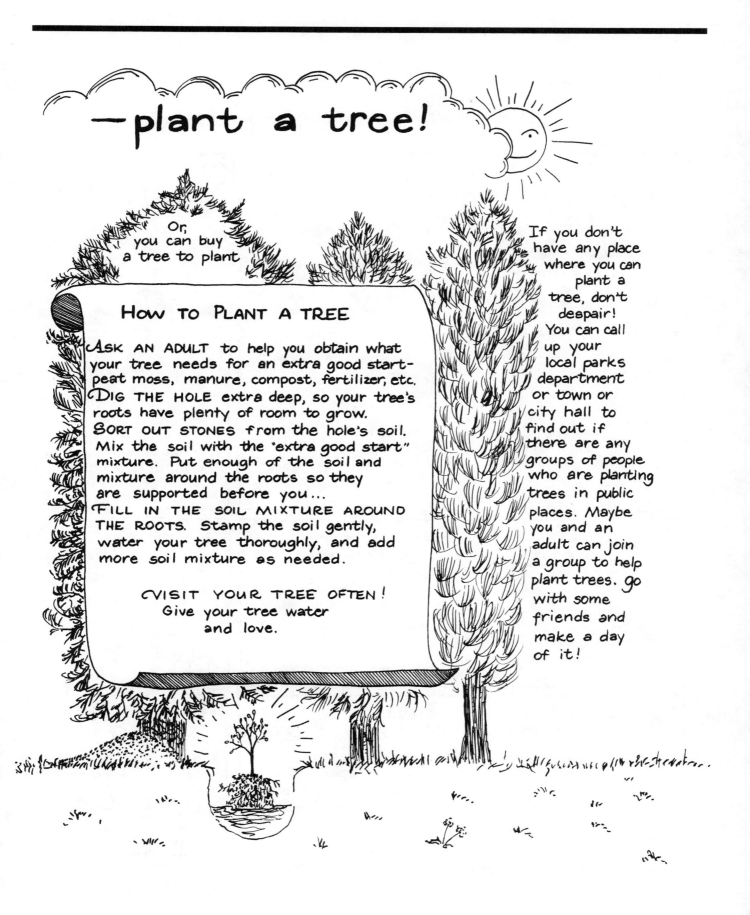

—plant a tree!

Or, you can buy a tree to plant

How to Plant a Tree

Ask an adult to help you obtain what your tree needs for an extra good start—peat moss, manure, compost, fertilizer, etc.

Dig the hole extra deep, so your tree's roots have plenty of room to grow.

Sort out stones from the hole's soil. Mix the soil with the "extra good start" mixture. Put enough of the soil and mixture around the roots so they are supported before you...

Fill in the soil mixture around the roots. Stamp the soil gently, water your tree thoroughly, and add more soil mixture as needed.

Visit your tree often! Give your tree water and love.

If you don't have any place where you can plant a tree, don't despair! You can call up your local parks department or town or city hall to find out if there are any groups of people who are planting trees in public places. Maybe you and an adult can join a group to help plant trees. go with some friends and make a day of it!

177

Sweatin' up a storm

(1)
On a hot sunny summer day, you drink a glass of soda.

(2)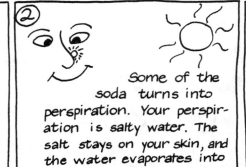
Some of the soda turns into perspiration. Your perspiration is salty water. The salt stays on your skin, and the water evaporates into the air.

(3) That night, "your drop of water" becomes a drop of dew after the sun goes down.

(7)
Rain falls. Your drop of water falls too.

(8) It soaks into the ground.

(9)
It becomes part of the groundwater for a while.

(13)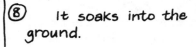
It rises again, to become part of another cloud.

(14) It becomes rain once again,

(15) this time to fall on a stream...
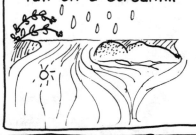

(19) The sun heats up the ocean waves.

(20) Your drop of water becomes water vapor once again, and rises into a big thunderhead cloud.

(21)
"A thunderstorm is expected to roll in this afternoon...."

THE WATER CYCLE

Here is a story about a bead of perspiration that formed on your nose one summer day. *It could be true!*

④

The next day, the sun evaporates the dew. Your drop of dew rises with the heated air as the day gets hotter.

⑤ It becomes part of a cloud.

⑥ The cloud joins up with other clouds. The sky gets dark.

⑩ An oak tree's root finds your water and thirstily sucks it up...

⑪

...through the trunk and into the leaves...

⑫ ...and the oak tree releases your drop of water as water vapor through its leaves on a sunny day.

⑯ which flows into a river...

⑰ ...which flows into a bigger river...

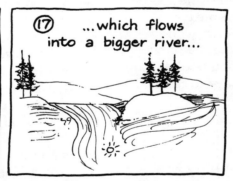

⑱ ...which flows into the ocean.

㉒ Your drop of water falls into a water reservoir.

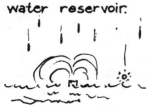

㉓

A soda company uses the water to make the soda...

㉔ ...that you drink on a hot sunny day the next summer!

179

Resources:
More Things to Do

How to Look at a Book

There is probably a book about almost any little part of the natural world. For example, are you interested in deer? Have you caught just a glimpse of a deer and wondered how he or she lives? Or maybe you would just like to look at pictures of deer.

You can find whole books that are written about deer, with pictures showing how they live. Some books have only one chapter about deer included among chapters about other kinds of animals. (A book about mammals might be arranged this way.)

Spend lots of time looking through books. Find pictures and read their captions (the words that tell about the pictures, often underneath them). Read a little bit here, a little bit there—whatever catches your eye. Remember: You don't have to read every word when you are reading for pleasure or to find some specific information. You're free as a bird!

And don't forget that the person who wrote the book probably loves what he or she has written about. In a way, a good book is a gift from its author, even if we have to return it to a library.

Where to Find Books

Libraries, of course, are great places to look for books about a subject you are interested in. You can use the card catalogue or ask a librarian to help you find those books about deer. Take a pile of books with you to a desk and flip through them. Take as long as you want, and choose the best ones to take home with you. A good book will let you wander through its pages the same way you wander around outdoors on an idle sunny day. You will learn something you did not know. And you will probably want to learn more.

How about bookstores? Of course they can be great places to find books, especially recently published books. You may be lucky enough to get a book you want as a gift, or you may be able to buy it yourself.

Or maybe your library has a book you saw in a bookstore. Even if it doesn't, a librarian may be able to order the book for you from another library, if you give him or her its title and author. Sometimes one library will agree to help other libraries find the books that library-goers want and need. So give it a try! You may have to wait a while until you see the book, but some books are worth waiting for.

Books and Other Ways to Learn

There are, as you know, books that are specifically about one subject (for example, deer). There are also books that are more general (for example, a book about mammals). There are several other kinds of books and other sources of information that you may be interested in, according to your needs.

Field Guides: These are books that are made for "taking into the field." They are a handy size for carrying and have pictures with matching descriptions to help you identify what you find outdoors.

There are field guides for wild flowers, rocks and minerals, sea shells, trees, and mammals. There are field guides for cloud shapes, reptiles and amphibians, insects and spiders, fish, and ferns.

There are field guides especially for children, and field guides for adults that you may find useful, even if you need an adult's help to learn how to use them.

To use a field guide, first you need to know how it is organized. Get to know how to use it. Do you find a picture first, then flip to the page number given in the caption to read about it? Or are the picture and the description together on the same page?

Nature Activities: There are books about science experiments and nature activities that are written for children. You'll know what you like when you see it!

There are also adult books about nature activities to do with a family or with a group of children. Maybe an adult in your life will be willing to borrow or buy a book or two so that you can do things together.

Nature Books for Adults: If you're really interested in something, don't be afraid to look at books about nature that are written for adults. The print may look like too much to read, but if there are some good pictures, why not give the book some of your time?

Natural History Magazines: A library will usually have several nature magazines on display. Look through current and back issues (this month's issue and magazines from before this month) for ideas and articles that interest you. *Ranger Rick, National Geographic World, Owl,* and *Your Big Backyard* are some "natural history" magazines.

Videotapes: If your library has a videotape collection, a librarian may be able to help you find videotapes on subjects that might interest you.

Records and Tapes: Did you know that people go out with microphones and collect all different kinds of sounds? You can find tapes and records that will help you to learn about bird songs and insect sounds. People have even gone out into jungles, beaches, or other wild places to make recordings of what those places sound like. Listening to the sounds of a field in, for example, the mountains of Pennsylvania early on a June morning can be a surprising treat in the middle of January.

Join Some Groups

Do you want to learn more about the outdoors than you can learn from your family? Some families go hiking and camping together, but others, for many reasons, may not want to or be able to spend time exploring outdoors together. Here are some groups you may want to think about joining:

- Boy Scouts of America or Girl Scouts of America
- Camp Fire Boys and Girls
- Science museum, aquarium, or zoological society classes for children
- Nature center classes for children
- Local parks programs, other community programs, or special hikes for children or families
- Outdoor clubs at school

Keep Your Ears Open

You can learn so much from other people! Friends of your family, neighbors, adults at school—many people know a lot about the natural world. Talk with them! Maybe your aunt knows a lot about birds and will take you to see migrating birds in the spring. Maybe a neighbor knows about wild plants and how they can be used as medicine. Wise people can be found in the most unlikely places. Maybe one of the people who makes school lunches is a fisherman and can tell you about fish. You never know unless you keep your ears open and ask questions. Don't be afraid to talk with people who know about and love the natural world.

List of Activities

Boldfaced letters following the page references indicate if the activity is appropriate for indoors (**I**) or outdoors (**O**).

Chapter 1   Trees

A Different Way to Color   6   **I**
How Do Plants Make Their Own Food?   9   **I**
What Is a Tree Saying to You?   12   **O**
How to Make a Bark Rubbing   14   **O**
How to Keep a Leaf   20–21   **I** and **O**
A Coconut Climb   23   **I**
What Kind of Tree Am I?   24   **I**

Chapter 2   Green Plants

Growing Beans   28   **I**
Burdock People   35   **I** or **O**
Leaves and Sun   38   **I** and **O**
Wildflower Seeds for Your Garden   39   **O**
Drawing Green Plants   40–41   **O**
Collecting Tiny Flowers   43   **O**
The Adaptation Game   44–45   **I**

Chapter 3   Soil

A Sandpaper Experiment   50   **I**
How to Draw a Mushroom   52   **O**
Sprouts   54   **I** and **O**
Measure a Nematode   57   **I**
How Can You See the World Beneath
   Your Feet?   58–59   **O**
Sow Bugs   60   **I** and **O**
Soil Erosion Experiment   61   **O**
Wormino's Wanderings   62–63   **I**

Chapter 4   Animals

Help This Woodchuck   69   **I**
Can You Read This Track Story?   76–77   **I**
Make Yourself a Pair of Deer Ears   78   **I** or **O**
Fast Eyes   80   **O**
Fawn Magic   83   **O**
How Does a Snail Move?   89   **I** and **O**
How to Become an Animal   91   **I**

Chapter 5   Birds

Mystery Drawing   97   **I**
Flying Paper, Flying Wings   99   **I**
Fluffy Birds   102–103   **I**
Start a Feather Collection   104   **I** and **O**
Figuring Out Feathers   105   **I**
Taking a Nest   110   **I** and **O**
Help Birds Build Their Nests   115   **O**
Draw a Flying Bird!   116   **I**
How to Help Out Backyard
   Birds   117   **I** and **O**
Word Bird   118–119   **I**

Chapter 6   Insects and Spiders

Catching Insects and Spiders   132–133   **O**
Keeping Insects and Spiders   134   **I** and **O**
Some Gall   135   **O**
Erasing an Ant Trail   139   **O**
Be a Bee   140   **I** or **O**
Bee Puzzled   141   **I**
The Difference Between Insects and
   Spiders   146–147   **I**
Are All Bugs the Same?   148   **I**

Chapter 7   Weather

How to Catch the Wind   158–159   **I** and **O**
Make Your Own Dew   160   **I** or **O**
Weather Facts   161   **I**
A Cricket Can Tell You the
   Temperature   169   **O**
The Chicory Challenge   170   **O**
Weather Walks   172–173   **O**
Change the Weather—Plant a
   Tree!   176–177   **O**

Index

A

Activities. *See* page 182 for a complete list
Adaptation
　of green plants, 37–39
　of insects, 128
Air
　humidity of, 154, 157
　moving of (wind), 157
　pressure of, in weather, 153–154
　in soil, 54
　temperature of, 155
　"Thinking about," 154
　trees and, 4–7
Amebas. *See* Protozoa
Animals, 65–94
　activities
　　"Can you read this track story?", 76–77
　　"Deer ears," 78
　　"Fast eyes," 80
　　"Fawn magic," 88
　　"Help this woodchuck," 69
　　"How does a snail move?", 89
　　"How to become an animal," 91
　amphibians, 84–86
　camouflage and, 73
　cold-blooded, 85
　decay and, 51
　fish, 86
　homes of, 72–73
　invertebrate, 89–90
　kingdom of, 67
　mammals as, 84
　people as, 90–92
　pollination and, 29
　reptiles, 87–89
　runs, 1, 74
　as seed dispersers, 35
　senses of, 79–82
　as soil makers, 54
　territories of, 70
　tracks of, 75–77
　vertebrates, 89
　as weather forecasters, 169
Ants, 56, 139

B

Bacteria, 50–51, 67
Bees, 41, 140–141

　honey, 139
　pollination and, 29–31
Birds, 95–119
　activities
　　"Draw a flying bird," 116
　　"Figuring out feathers," 105
　　"Fluffy birds," 102–103
　　"Flying paper, flying wings," 99
　　"Helping birds build nests," 115
　　"How to help out backyard birds," 117
　　"Mystery drawing," 97
　　"Start a feather collection," 104
　　"Taking a nest," 110
　　"Word bird," 118–119
　beaks of, 107–109
　body language of, 109
　feathers of, 96–105
　feet of, 107
　migration of, 111–114
　nests of, 110, 115
　voices of, 109
Butterflies, 146, 168–169

C

Cactus, 19, 24, 37
Camouflage, of animals, 73
Carbon dioxide, 6, 7, 9
Cerci, 131
Chicory, 169, 170
Chitin, 123
Chlorophyll, 8
Classification
　of animals, 67
　of bacteria, 67
　of fungi, 51
Clouds, 162–167
Clover, 40
Crickets, 144, 169

D

Dandelions, 26, 33, 36, 46
Decay, 50–53
Dew, 160
Dirt. *See* soil
Dragonflies, 129, 145

E

Erosion, 60–61
Exoskeletons, of insects, 90, 123, 125–126, 147

F

Feathers
　collecting of, 104
　molting of, 101
　preening of, 106
　structure of, 96–98, 103–105
　types of, 98–101
Flagellates. *See* Protozoa
Flies, 142
Fruit, 22, 32–34
Flowers, 27
　collecting, 43
　pollination and, 29–30
　shapes of, 45
　on trees, 22
Frost, 160
Fungus, 50–51

G

Galls, 135
Grasshoppers, 129–130, 144
Green plants, 25–46
　activities
　　"Adaptation game," 44–45
　　"Burdock people," 35
　　"Collecting tiny flowers," 43
　　"Drawing green plants," 40–41
　　"Growing beans," 28
　　"Leaves and sun," 38
　　"Wildflower seeds for your garden," 39
　making own food, 8–9
　medicine and, 41
　as weather forecasters, 169–170

H

Honey guides, 31
Humidity, 157
Hygrometers, 174

I

Insects, 121–148
　activities
　　"Are all bugs the same?", 148
　　"Be a bee," 140
　　"Bee puzzled," 141
　　"Catching insects," 132–133
　　"The difference between insects and spiders," 146–147
　　"Erasing an ant trail," 139

"Keeping insects," 134
"Some gall," 135
chrysalis or cocoon of, 00
eating leaves, 39
galls and, 135
larvae of, 126
metamorphosis of, 125–126
molting of, 123, 125–126, 147
pollination and, 29–31, 142
pupae of, 56, 126
senses of, 128–131
in soil, 56
structure of, 124
as weather forecasters, 168–169

L

Ladybugs, 137
Leaves, 15–17, 20–21, 45
Lichen, 48
Lightning, 166–167

M

Mammals, 84, 90; *see also* Animals
Metamorphosis, of insects, 125–127
Meteorologists, 150
Migration of birds, 111–114
Molting
of feathers, 101
of insects' exoskeletons, 123–126
Mosquitoes, 143
Moths, 130, 146
Mushrooms, 51, 52

N

Native Americans, 22, 33, 143
Nectar, 29, 30
Nematodes, 57

O

Ornithologists, 112
Oxygen, 5–9, 41

P

Plants. *See* Green plants
Poison ivy, 41–42
Pollination
by animals, 29–31
by insects, 32, 140, 142
by wind, 32

Plantains, 26
Protozoa, 57

R

Rain, 160
Rocks, 48–50
Roots, 13, 45

S

Seeds
dispersal, 33–35
growing, 20, 27–28, 39
Senses
of animals, 78–82
of insects, 128–131
Snow, 162
Soil, 47–63
activities
"How can you see the world
beneath your feet?", 58–59
"How to draw a mushroom,"
52
"Measure a nematode," 57
"A sandpaper experiment," 50
"Soil erosion experiment," 61
"Sow bugs and soil," 60
"Sprouting soil," 54
animals and, 54
classifying of, 58
erosion and, 60–61
fungus and bacteria in, 50, 51, 53
green plants and, 41, 50–51, 53
insects in, 56
judging health of, 48
life depends on, 48, 60–61
nematodes and protozoa in, 57
rocks in, 48–50
sow bugs and, 59, 60
Spiders, 56, 136–138, 169
difference from insects, 146–147
structure of, 137
webs of, 138
Sunlight
helping plants to make food, 8–9
leaves and, 38

T

Territories
of animals, 70
of birds, 109

of crickets and cicadas, 130
Tracks of animals, 75–77
Trees, 3–24
activities
"A coconut climb," 23
"A different way to color," 6
"How do plants make their
own food?", 9
"How to keep a leaf," 20–21
"How to make a bark rubbing,"
14
"What does a tree say to you?",
12
"What kind of tree am I?", 24
broadleaf, 18, 24
conifer, 18, 24
making own food, 8
palm, 19, 24
roots, 13
water and, 19

V

Vertebrates, 89

W

Water
condensation of, 157
cycle of, 178–179
helping trees to make own food,
8–9
plants growing in, 39
vaporizing of, 157
Weather, 149–179
activities
"Change the weather—plant a
tree!", 176–177
"Chicory challenge," 170
"A cricket can tell you the
temperature," 169
"How to catch the wind," 158
"Make your own dew," 160
"Weather facts," 161
"Weather walks," 172
people and, 174–178
prediction of, 150–152, 163–178
Weeds, 41
Wind, 157, 158–159
Woodchucks, 54, 55, 71–72